The Mind

The Mind

Into the Inner World

TORSTAR BOOKS
New York ● Toronto

TORSTAR BOOKS INC.
41 Madison Avenue, Suite 2900
New York, NY 10010

THE HUMAN BODY
The Mind:
Into the Inner World

Publisher
Bruce Marshall

Art Editor
John Bigg

Creation Coordinator
Harold Bull

Editor
John Clark

Managing Editor
Ruth Binney

Commissioning Editor
Hal Robinson

Contributors
Adrian Furnham, Sue Henley, Peter Howell, Steve Parker, Peter Salmon, Chris Thompson, Cathy Weir

Text Editors
Wendy Allen, Mike Darton, Lloyd Lindo, Maria Pal

Researchers
Angela Bone, Jazz Wilson

Picture Researchers
Jan Croot, Dee Robinson

Layout and Visualization
Rita Wuthrich

Artists
Mick Gillah, Aziz Khan, Yann le Goaec, Mick Saunders, Shirley Willis

Cover Design
Moonink Communications

Cover Art
Paul Giovanopoulos

Production Director
Barry Baker

Production Coordinator
Janice Storr

Business Coordinator
Candy Lee

Planning Assistant
Avril Essery

International Sales
Barbara Anderson

In conjunction with this series Torstar Books offers an electronic digital thermometer which provides accurate body temperature readings in large liquid crystal numbers within 60 seconds.

For more information write to:
Torstar Books Inc.
41 Madison Avenue, Suite 2900
New York, NY 10010

Marshall Editions, an editorial group that specializes in the design and publication of scientific subjects for the general reader, prepared this book. Marshall has written and illustrated standard works on technology, animal behavior, computer usage and the tropical rain forests which are recommended for schools and libraries as well as for popular reference.

Series Consultants
Donald M. Engelman is Professor of Molecular Biophysics and Biochemistry and Professor of Biology at Yale. He has pioneered new methods for understanding cell membranes and ribosomes, and has also worked on the problem of atherosclerosis. He has published widely in professional and lay journals and lectured at many universities and international conferences. He is also involved with National Advisory Groups concerned with Molecular Biology, Cancer, and the operation of National Laboratory Facilities.

Stanley Joel Reiser is Professor of Humanities and Technology in Health Care at the University of Texas Health Science Center in Houston. He is the author of *Medicine and the Reign of Technology*, coeditor of *Ethics in Medicine: Historical Perspectives and Contemporary Concerns*, and coeditor of the anthology *The Machine at the Bedside*.

Harold C. Slavkin, Professor of Biochemistry at the University of Southern California, directs the Graduate Program in Craniofacial Biology and also serves as Chief of the Laboratory for Developmental Biology in the University's Gerontology Center. His research on the genetic basis of congenital defects of the head and neck has been widely published.

Lewis Thomas is Chancellor of the Memorial Sloan-Kettering Cancer Center in New York City and University Professor at the State University of New York, Stony Brook. A member of the National Academy of Sciences, Dr. Thomas has served on advisory councils of the National Institutes of Health.

Consultants for The Mind
Phillip Lee is a cofounder of Psychiatric Consultation Associates, a group specializing in the interface of medicine and psychiatry. He is a clinical affiliate of The New York Hospital and is Clinical Instructor in Psychiatry at Cornell University Medical Center. Dr. Lee served as a consultant for *The Brain* in The Human Body series. He is also engaged in the practice of psychiatry in New York City.

Susan Tross is Clinical Assistant Psychologist at Payne Whitney Psychiatric Clinic, Cornell University Medical College, New York. Her coauthored publications have included articles concerned with the psychological aspects of certain types of cancer and their therapy, and neuropsychological and psychosocial factors involved in acquired immunodeficiency syndrome (AIDS). She has also been Coordinator of projects for the National Cancer Institute and the National Institute of Mental Health.

Medical Advisor
Arthur Boylston

© Torstar Books Inc. 1985

**Library of Congress
Cataloging in Publication Data**

Main entry under title:

The Mind : into the inner world.

Includes index.
1. Intellect. 2. Brain. [DNLM:
1. Brain—physiology—popular works.
2. Psychophysiology—popular works.
WL 103 M6625]
BF431.M525   1986   153   86-1405

ISBN 0-920269-22-2 (The Human Body Series)
ISBN 0-920269-98-2 (The Mind)
ISBN 1-55001-002-6 (leatherbound)
ISBN 0-920269-93-1 (school ed.)

20 19 18 17 16 15 14 13 12 11
10 9 8 7 6 5 4 3 2 1

Printed in Belgium

Contents

**Introduction:
Making Up Your Mind** 7

1 **What is the Mind?** 9

2 **The Developing Mind** 33

3 **Thinking and Learning** 61

4 **A Meeting of Minds** 89

5 **The Hidden Self** 105

6 **Modifying Behavior** 125

Glossary 152
Illustration Credits 156
Index 157

Introduction:

Making Up Your Mind

It has become fashionable to think we know a lot about the mind. The development of psychology over the last century is reckoned to be evidence toward this — and indeed it is true that psychologists can often tell us why we think this and why we dislike that, and psychiatrists can help us lose our less rational loves and hates. "Amateur psychology" is rife, as are the manipulative methods used by advertising agencies and sales personnel. The study of communications — semantics, semiotics — has also come on apace, to the extent that even if psychology has not yet been reduced to a code of universal rules and statements, the study of linguistics has made strenuous attempts to become just that, even in relation to communication with non-humans. The mind is said also to be significant in art, and ought to be supremely important in philosophy, suggesting that creativity is another functionally significant aspect of the mind.

And yet how much of this reflects more the functions of the brain than those of the mind? There is a difference: the mind is to some degree dependent on the proper functioning of the brain, but otherwise could be said to make use of the brain's facilities relatively independently. If the brain malfunctions, so does the mind, yet in normal circumstances surely the mind *uses* the brain to think, to create? Is it the mind or the brain that can be trained — and is "lateral thinking" training the mind or brain to think in an untrained way?

Certainly, the brain is the physical site of whatever the mind is. But what *is* the mind? Is it the "self," the essential "you"? The mind can be considered as the aspect of you that "operates" the brain, that makes the decisions (based on the brain's information), that makes use of the brain's knowledge and memories, that feels the emotions and may undergo religious experiences, that is at once the most human and most superhuman part of you. Yet nobody really knows what it is that makes up your mind.

"O the mind, mind has mountains; cliffs of fall, frightful, sheer, no-man-fathomed," wrote the eminent cleric Gerard Manley Hopkins. Another religious poet, William Blake, produced this image of divine computation, entitled The Ancient of Days, *representing so aptly that irrepressible human desire: to gauge the fathomless depths of the mind — a task in which science and religion are commensurately engaged.*

7

Chapter 1

What is the Mind?

The human mind is arguably the summit of the evolutionary process to date. Minds and bodies of *Homo sapiens*, working in tandem, have reshaped our planetary home, earth, and are the key to its future. The individual human mind is the powerhouse of all culture, which is itself created by communication between many minds. This communication is made possible largely by the use of visual and vocal symbols to represent thoughts and objects. Symbols can be fairly literal representations of objects, such as drawings, or complex combinations of individual ciphers (letters), in themselves abstract and standing for abstract concepts such as justice. All poetry, drama, art and science, all technology and almost all of the way the world looks today, would not exist unless the human mind had evolved from non-thinking matter.

Humans have always been capable of logical thought and this, more than any other attribute, sets us apart from most other creatures. Early historical evidence that mankind was capable of reflecting upon the nature of his own mind came in about 430 B.C. with the work of the Greek philosopher Anaxagoras. For Anaxagoras, mind (*nous* in Greek) was a substance which entered into some objects and made them alive, a sort of "life force." He considered that humans were raised above the level of animals not by their extra intelligence or the possession of a mind, however, but by the possession of hands with which to express the contents of the mind. Aristotle and Socrates, later Greek philosophers, complained that after Anaxagoras invented the mind he made very little use of it.

From this early beginning, mankind's reflections on the nature of himself have had a mystical quality — and, from a Western point of view, nowhere more evidently than in the East. In Chinese Taoism, man's mind, like earth and heaven, was thought to be made up of the two opposing principles Yin and Yang, and the five

Light and dark, heaven and hell, masculine and feminine, madness and sanity — human beings have long thought in terms of opposites. The ancient Chinese symbols of Yin and Yang (literally, the dark and sunny side of a hill) — shown here on a protective amulet — represent these opposites existing in a harmonious balance. The symbols aptly represent the aims of modern psychology — firstly to understand how the normal, balanced mind works, and secondly, to restore a healthy balance in patients suffering from mental disturbance.

elements of wood, fire, soil, metal and water. Yin is the dark, negative, passive principle and Yang is the light, positive active one that balances it. At about the same time in Greece, Plato was categorizing man and the world similarly into earth, air, fire and water. Through to the Middle Ages and beyond, personality was thought to be determined by the predominance of one type of body fluid — either black or yellow bile, blood or phlegm — over the other "elements of life."

Inevitably, an understanding of what constitutes the human mind and how it differs from that of animals is crucial to an understanding not only of ourselves as individuals, but also of the human condition in general.

Knowing and Perceiving

Central to the idea of mind is the act of knowing. Philosophers through the ages have occupied themselves with the question: How do we know? How do I know that the tree over there is green? How do I know that it is a tree, and not a mirage? If the tree falls in a storm and there is nobody there to hear it crash to the ground — does it make a noise? These are forms of the same question: How am I conscious of things around me, things that are separate from me?

This is an extremely difficult question even for the philosophers, although few others bother to ask it. The Stoic Greek philosophers held that knowledge was perception, which does not leave much room for abstract knowledge such as the meaning of the word "justice"; their approach was vigorously refuted by Plato.

How do we know that the things we see and hear are really there? The answer is, of course, that we do not; we may be having a hallucination. Evidence of our correctness derives from the fact that we are usually correct in our predictions. For example, on countless occasions during a lifetime we see something and then reach out toward the place where we see it. Virtually always we touch it when we expect to, and we may also smell it or hear it making a noise. This experience of an object's being experienced by many senses at once gives it reality. But to many philosophers this has not always seemed a sufficient answer. Our faculties can be fooled, as magicians and illusionists have shown through the ages, and as even we ourselves experience. You cannot necessarily believe your eyes — or ears, nose, tongue or fingers.

From Descartes to Darwin

The English Bishop George Berkeley (1685–1753) tried to solve the entire question of the relationship of mind to the outside world by saying that things themselves exist only when they are being observed by us. In other words, the mind does not just reflect the world around us, it actually keeps it going. How, then, do objects stay in the same place from one observation to the next? What gives the world its apparent constancy? Berkeley had a clever answer to this, as expressed in the following lines by another English churchman, Ronald Knox:

> *There was a young man who said "God*
> *Must think it exceedingly odd*
> *If he finds that the tree*
> *Continues to be*
> *When there's no one about in the quad."*

The reply was:

> *Dear Sir, your astonishment's odd:*
> *I am always about in the quad,*
> *And that's why the tree*
> *Continues to be*
> *Since observed by, yours faithfully,*
> GOD.

(The "quad," as you might guess, is a college quadrangle.) From a modern standpoint this "solution" is obviously one of those philosophers' tricks which bears little relation to reality.

One influential philosopher of the seventeenth century who adopted a similar position, though not so extreme, was the French mathematician, scientist and all-round genius René Descartes (1596–1650). He lived in an age when the Church was extremely powerful and, like the Italian scientist Galileo in the field of astronomy, he ran the risk of falling foul of that institution by contradicting its dogma in his theories. He welcomed the demonstration by the English physician William Harvey of the circulation of the blood around the body, one of the greatest advances in medicine and the final nail in the coffin of the theory that the mind resided in the heart. (The Greek physician Hippocrates, nearly twenty centuries earlier, was convinced that this was wrong, but the ignorant continued to believe it.)

Descartes started from the sound scientific principle that everything is open to doubt until proved. Our own human senses can be tricked and so should be doubted, and one cannot build a philosophy on the basis of the information they provide. The only sound reference point in Descartes' world was thought. "I think, therefore I am," he said; a phrase which has echoed down the ages. (In fact, because he wrote in Latin, his actual words were: *Cogito, ergo sum.*) The mind was thus the starting point and more real than anything else. I exist only while I think; if I cease to think, there would be no evidence of my existence.

Like the great English scientist Isaac Newton, who invented his own mathematics to explain his advances in physics and mechanics, Descartes intended eventually to create a philosophy and a picture of the universe in which everything would be explained mechanically. If the mind did exist separately from the body, what sort of thing could it be? Where is it, and what are its properties? What Descartes could not explain — and what we still cannot explain today — is what the mind is and how it can interact with or influence the body. Conversely, how is it that the body can also influence the mind?

Descartes' idea of the mind was an object, a physical entity, but one which took up no space. How could such a thing move a limb? Descartes invented a wholly spurious system in which the soul or mind moved "vital forces" about in the brain by its action on a special organ called the pineal, chosen because of its position in the center of the brain. We now know that the pineal is in fact a hormonal gland, derived from a type of primitive third eye, although Descartes thought it was a kind of muscle.

It is hardly surprising that Descartes could not discover how the mind and body interact. Scientists still do not completely know. Even Descartes'

12

Is the mind a "ghost in the machine" as the British philosopher Gilbert Ryle disparagingly believed, or is human consciousness merely the result of electrical and chemical activity in the brain? Are human beings, if not clockwork machines, no more than biological computers? Despite scientific knowledge of many areas of the brain and its processes, the idea remains that the mind is an addition to the physical self or body.

own followers did not believe his theory that the mind acted on the body through the pineal. The German philosopher Gottfried Leibniz (1646–1716) — who according to Bertrand Russell in his *History of Western Philosophy* was one of the nicest philosophers — tried to get round this problem. He proposed that the mind and the body do not interact at all. They are really quite distinct.

How is it, then, that when you are embarrassed you blush? Surely it is the mental embarrassment, in the mind, that interacts with the body's physiology to make your cheeks red? No, says Leibniz. In the universe are two clocks which are perfectly accurate. One drives mental events and the other controls physical events. They were both set off by God at the same time and so your body and your mind run entirely separately, but God has ensured that things always happen with perfect timing in each sphere, thus giving rise to the illusion that one causes the other.

Many such philosophies were bandied about, with little evidence of a firm framework or direction, until the English naturalist Charles Darwin (1809–1882) came along with his theory of evolution. To Darwin and many other scientists it became unwise to base theory totally upon the existence — or otherwise — of God. The universe took another materialistic turn and followers of Leibniz suddenly went out of fashion. Darwin placed the study of the mind firmly in the biologists' camp, and wrote a book entitled *The Expression of the Emotions in Man and Animals*, based on evolutionary theory.

Today's Philosophy

The weight of scientific evidence is firmly in favor of the notion that nearly everything going on in the mind is based on events occurring in the brain. Modern studies of the effects of damage to particular areas of the brain suggest that different parts of

Human beings have always sought to understand the nature of mind and personality. Astrological explanations (below left), in which the planets (symbolized on the man's head) influenced behavior and

emotions, have been widely accepted for many centuries — and some people still hold to them today. Astrology has no scientific basis, but like works of literature it may help people to understand themselves

better. Harder evidence of how the brain works or malfunctions may be obtained by brain scan techniques (below right). Here, the brain's structure is being mapped. The small screen shows a cross-section.

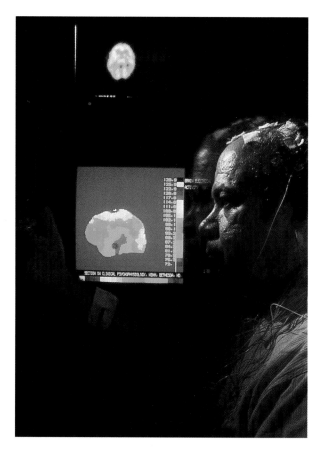

the brain are associated with different mental functions, such as memory, speech and the ability to draw; this is termed localization. However, each localized function occurs within the context of the integrated action of the brain as a whole, and therefore requires the mediation of other brain functions. In other words, the brain is the principal organ of the mind.

Many twentieth-century philosophers, in particular the Englishman Gilbert Ryle, have taken the view that the idea of "mind" is a myth. They say that if what goes on in the mind is based only on a series of chemical reactions and electrical signals in the brain, then surely we no longer need even to begin to talk about outdated concepts such as the mind.

In order to discuss the mind, therefore, it is necessary to accept a compromise: the idea of the mind is a reality, but at the same time it is dependent on the brain. How is the mind itself constructed? What are the attributes by which the mind alone can be described?

The Psychological Revolution

Not until the eighteenth and nineteenth centuries did the mind become a serious object of scientific study. This came about partly because, in the nineteenth century, with the increasing organization of society, there was a heightened awareness of those people who were unable to fit in because of some abnormality of mind, either lunacy or idiocy (to use terms of the day). More sophisticated technology, the publication of the theory of evolution and the growing confidence that there were no limits to human understanding — if applied in the right way — led scientists and biologists, as well as philosophers, into the study of the mind. Later, some of them specialized in this area and became psychologists.

Early in the psychological revolution of the

The introduction of computer technology has led to the use of new analogies to describe the way in which the mind operates. Experiences can be thought of as the input, the raw material that we process. The mind has its memory banks too and some ready-built programs that cause people to react in the ways that they do. As computer technology advances, could machine and man become equally skilled?

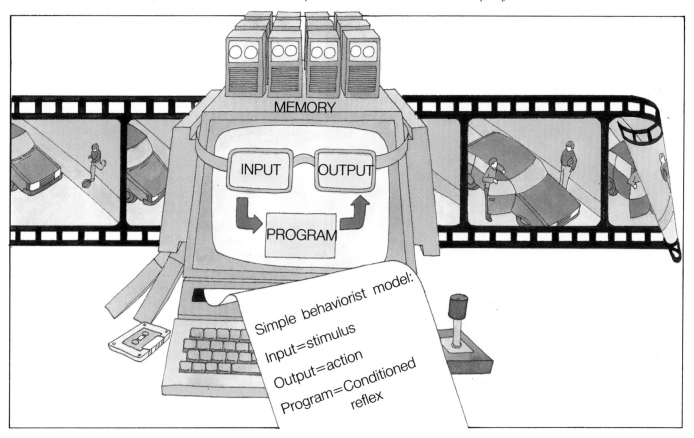

Simple behaviorist model:

Input=stimulus

Output=action

Program=Conditioned reflex

nineteenth century came the phrenologists. For them the mind was composed of several aptitudes. In retrospect the qualities of mind which they chose as important appear rather odd: poetry, love of food, sense of size and sense of causality. Each of these aptitudes was said to correspond to a bump on the surface of the skull, so that a phrenologist (the greatest of whom was the German physician Franz Josef Gall) could feel the skull and tell which parts of a person's mind were most highly developed.

This entire theory was based on nothing more than supposition; as neurology (the scientific study of the brain and nerves) advanced, people came to realize how little value there was in phrenology, so it gradually died out.

One of the most influential of the early psychologists, a man who was also the most eminent American philosopher of his time, was William James (1842–1910). James touched various aspects of psychology from mental disorder to religious experience. Perhaps the best known of his contributions was his theory of emotion, which challenged previously accepted theories in this area. Psychologists had, up to that time, argued that when we experience something and are frightened, we run away because we are frightened. In other words, emotions are the mental causes of actions. James disagreed. He said that we are afraid because we run. In other words, it is felt emotion that is the result of physiological arousal and activity. He argued that we are activated by complicated reflexes and we infer our emotions on the basis of physiological arousal and cognition. Modern experiments in psychology have given some support to this view. This focus on observable, functional aspects of human behavior is called functionalism. Functionalism was the forerunner of behaviorism. This discipline views the minds of animals, and those of humans, as bun-

The American psychologist Burrhus F. Skinner (1904–) extended Pavlov's concept of conditioning. He described behavior that is learned because of consequences that follow it — rather than due to stimuli that precede it. When animals have nothing to do, they still move about and explore. Sometimes their actions produce consequences they can use to their own advantage. For example, if they turn over a stone there might be something good underneath to eat. If there is, then the probability of turning over another stone in the near future will be increased. This is called "operant conditioning," which implies that an item of behavior is repeated if it is rewarded or reinforced.

Extrapolating from the results of experiments on laboratory animals such as rats, Skinner vigorously argued that behaviorist theories could be directly applied to all human beings. In his book *Beyond Freedom and Dignity*, he argues that the concept of free will is fiction and the modus operandi for all individual behavior is to use behavioral reinforcement to exact desired results from others. What is not spelled out is precisely who does the conditioning and who is supposed to be conditioned.

Behaviorism is of major importance but, by being limited to observable behavior, tends to ignore internal mental processes which may mediate behavior. For example, to the question "What is a rewarding event?" the answer has to depend upon the interpretation placed upon the event by the individual. That interpretation is a mental event and is therefore not one the behaviorists would normally choose to study.

Differences Between Minds

In spite of the failure of phrenology, the young science of psychology was interested in defining its territory and began trying to map, in a more scientific way, the specific functions of the human mind. A pioneer in this field was the English scientist and relative of Darwin, Francis Galton (1822–1911).

Galton began the study of individual differences in mental as well as physical attributes. He studied families which had contributed several men of genius to science or art, in order to show the influence of heredity on these attributes. So began a debate about the relative contributions of "nature

dles of reflexes. The animal responds to stimuli with reflex actions. Gradually, the animal repeats these actions whenever it is in the presence of the same stimuli. This process, known as conditioning, is the foundation upon which behaviorism is based. For behaviorists, only observable behavior (governed by experimentally demonstrable laws) is the basis of psychological theory. The mind is regarded as a black box which cannot be experimentally manipulated. The American John B. Watson (1878–1958) was the founder of behaviorism; the other two major proponents were Pavlov and Skinner.

Ivan Pavlov (1849–1936), the Russian physiologist, was responsible for the idea of a psychological conditioning, although simple physical knee-jerk-type reflexes had been known for some time. He gave food to dogs and found that they salivated before eating it. This is a reflex starting from the smell and sight of food, and ending with the activation of the salivary glands. He then rang a bell every time he presented the food, and eventually the dogs associated the sound of the bell with the food and salivated when the bell rang — even when there was no food. Pavlov called this a "conditioned reflex." This type of conditioning has become known as classical conditioning.

William James

Pragmatic Psychologist-Philosopher

A great philosopher, a writer of vivid and imaginative prose, an innovative psychologist — William James was all these and an enigma too. The effects of his work in the field of psychology have been likened to those of Galileo in physics or Darwin in biology: fundamental, if limited by current standards of progress. In philosophy, James established the notion of pragmatism — that in a world of change (and sometimes very subtle or gradual change at that) and chance, the only grounds for belief are through active experience, experiment or research, and that in such a shifting and unpredictable world the one specific history-making ''event'' is the individual.

Born in New York City in January 1842, James was brought up in what some would now consider an oppressively intellectual and transitory household. His father was a strange and loquacious man of wide knowledge and sharp wit, an author with a vigorous writing style, who dragged his family back and forth across Europe and the United States, thus committing William's education to frequent interruptions.

This upbringing may have been peculiar, and was possibly also responsible for much of the ill health he suffered until his

mid-thirties. (It was probably unhelpful, too, to his brother, the famous novelist Henry James.) It nevertheless saw him equipped to study medicine at the Harvard Medical School in 1862, to go with Louis Agassiz as assistant in the celebrated exploration of the Amazon River, and then to travel to Germany to study with such eminent scientists as Hermann von Helmholtz, Rudolf Virchow and Claude Bernard. He then returned to become Doctor of Medicine at Harvard in 1869.

By then he was ill, however, and unable to practice his chosen profession; he read widely, attributing his eventual recovery to a new, more determined outlook on life.

From 1872, James's main interest was psychology, and he contracted with a publisher to produce a psychology textbook in two years. It actually took him twelve — but the work, *The Principles of Psychology* (1890), was a monumental classic, taking the field from the theoretical far into the practical, from the esoteric to the purely scientific.

But at that point James decided he'd had enough psychology; next he would concentrate on religious ideals. And from 1893 to 1903 he published several books and papers solely on the theme that religious experience is the same for all people — the same psychological event — no matter which religion is practiced.

Having made a completely new reputation for himself in that field, he then abandoned it in turn in favor of philosophy. It was in the subsequent few years that he established the concept of pragmatism, a scientific approach to analysis and the experience of meaningfulness. Philosophy in America, contemporarily stultified, was rejuvenated by the debate over his theories. His lectures and classes became famous for their crowded and lively nature. He died in August, 1910 at home in Chocorua, New Hampshire.

The Eysenck model of personality has two scales, one ranging from stability to neuroticism, the other from introversion to extroversion. Shown here as a chessboard, an individual's rating is determined by the answers he or she gives to a psychological questionnaire. But critics argue that such a system is unable to reflect the full complexity and subtlety of human personality that is apparent even in babies.

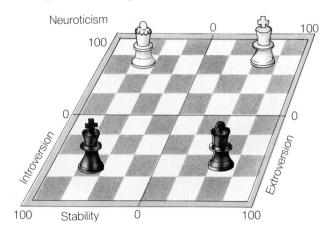

=75 Introversion/75 Neurotic
Anxious, withdrawn personality

=75 Extroversion/75 Neurotic
Attention-seeking personality

=75 Extroversion/75 Stable
Outgoing, capable personality

=75 Introversion/75 Stable
Meticulous, responsible personality

and nurture," or heredity and environment, to mental ability that has occupied a central place throughout the history of psychology.

Galton and his contemporaries initiated experimental techniques to quantify individual differences — known as the ideographic method. Based on these measurement techniques, the British psychologist Charles Spearman (1863–1945) proposed the two-factor theory of intelligence. According to this theory, intelligence is said to include a general factor, or "g" (which is required for all intellectual tasks), and a specific ability, known as factor "s."

After this general factor of ability there appears to be a hierarchy of lower-order abilities. At the most basic level of specificity, two types of ability may be distinguished — verbal ability and visuo-spatial or constructional ability — the ability to draw, for instance. Interestingly, this dichotomy, which was found by simply observing and analyzing differences between people, has been confirmed as more became known about the brain. Roughly, the left side of the brain deals with verbal and related abilities, and the right with visuo-spatial abilities.

Louis Thurstone (1887–1955), an American psychologist, proposed the group-factor theory of intelligence, which pinpointed several specific "primary mental abilities." Although Galton and his followers made important progress in the understanding of intelligence, they left a very large part of the mind untouched. That is the area of emotion, personality and the "experience of the self" that is so important in the philosophers' definitions of the difference between the human mind and the animal mind.

Measuring Personality

In the middle of the present century, psychologists began to use statistical methods, known as factor analysis, to explain the structure of personality. After measuring various characteristics in large groups of people, they identified a few key traits that described those people. The work of James Cattell (1860–1944) in the United States and of Hans Eysenck in Britain are important examples of

this approach. Starting with his laboratory studies of reaction times, Cattell pioneered the use of standard tests to measure individual differerences in mental abilities. Eysenck proposed that human personality could be described on three dimensions. As shown in the diagram on page 18, each dimension could be represented as an axis — with opposite attributes at either extreme and increasing values of the dimension between them.

However, the distillation of only a few dimensions of personality from studies of large numbers of people represents only one major trend in the development of psychology. Another key landmark in this development was the emergence of the psychoanalytical theory of the human mind. This was based not on the study of many people, but on the intensive study of a few individuals.

The Psychoanalyst's View of the Mind

The founder of psychoanalysis was Sigmund Freud (1856–1939). Beginning at the end of the nineteenth century, he developed his view of the mind by studying patients with nervous disorders.

'There's nothing I can do for you—you *are* a duck.'

Children play together happily, but according to Freud some childhood experiences have a profound effect in later life. With most patients referred to him, Freud uncovered a traumatic childhood event. On closer investigation, this event often proved to be imaginary — but it was no less painful for that. From this Freud postulated that neuroses are caused by the repression of natural instincts in children.

Many were suffering from what was then termed hysteria, a condition in which physical illness appears to be present although there is nothing detectably wrong with the patient's body. To circumvent this paradox, Freud used the already existing (but not much recognized) concept of an unconscious mind.

Originally, Freud divided the mind into three parts: the conscious, preconscious and unconscious. In the unconscious mind he located all the impulses, ideas, desires and images that the owner cannot cope with, or finds unacceptable. The process by which the once-conscious idea is submerged into the repository of the unconscious is called repression, or denial. Subsequently, Freud called three subdivisions of the mind the Id, the Ego and the Superego.

The Id was the part of the mind housing all those instinctual urges, desires and energies that drive behavior, governed by the pleasure principle. These, he stated, were either sexual or aggressive. Later he divided the urges located in the Id into two: the life instinct, Eros, and the death instinct, Thanatos. (Compare this idea with the Taoist view of Yin and Yang, the two opposing principles mentioned previously.)

The Id governs the mind of the infant. However, by interaction with the outside world, and particularly with the mother, the child gradually becomes a separate person who is able to control some of these urges by defense mechanisms, in much the same way as repression.

The new part of the mind which takes control as the child grows is called the Ego, which is governed by the reality principle. It is mostly composed of those thoughts of which we are aware, or can become aware of by an effort of will. This Ego becomes trained and socialized more and more until society's rules are fully assimilated. The third part of the mind is then created, which contains the rules and punishes the self for transgressions. It is called the Superego, which in Freudian thought is crystallized by the resolution of the Oedipal conflict.

Masks free people to express a part of their personality that would normally lie hidden. The madman who believes himself king (bottom) *may be doing the same thing — playing a role to express his deeper feelings.*

Freud's view of the mind has been criticized as unscientific, but his theory has nevertheless been extremely influential in modern thinking, not only on psychologists and psychiatrists (those who treat mental illness) but more so on philosophers, artists and historians.

Neo-Freudian Psychoanalysis

After Freud came a host of neo-Freudian psychoanalysts and philosophers, each with a slightly different interpretation of Freud's work based on his or her own experiences with generally neurotic patients.

One of the best known of these was Carl Jung (1875–1961), a Swiss psychiatrist who became an analyst. His synthesis was termed individual psychology; he postulated that the human mind is composed of "archetypes," or imagery, which are common to all cultures. For instance, the witch of children's dreams and stories is a universal symbol of the angry, bad, frightened mother. Austrian physician Alfred Adler (1870–1937), another of Freud's early disciples, invented the term "inferiority complex" and started a school known as ego psychology which gave more importance to conscious functions in the mind and less to unconscious factors.

Melanie Klein (1882–1960) was the originator of the so-called object-relations school of psychoanalysis. The term "object" is used to describe other people, either real or imagined, with whom the individual is emotionally involved. Object-relations theory emphasizes the pursuit of interpersonal relationships and personal identity, rather than instinctual gratification, as the basis of human motivation.

Psychoanalytic theory has been criticized by scientists because its methods do not conform to the traditional methods of hard science. Instead of setting up theories and systematically testing their truth — which is the proper scientific method — many psychoanalysts have tended to rely solely on personal intuition. It has been attacked for claiming to explain everything — virtually assuming the divine authority of a religion. No wonder the great scientific philosopher Karl Popper (1902–) says that analysts are convinced of the rightness of their creed. Nevertheless, although not all

Scientists hold a theory to be true — and scientific — if it is useful and cannot be shown to be false. The philosopher Karl Popper's objection to psychoanalytic theories is that there is no conceivable test which can be devised to prove them false. For example, the theory: "All swans are white," seems to be backed up by observing swans. But in Australia that theory is utterly confounded — some of the swans there are black.

Freud's theory of the Id, Ego and Superego may be useful to analysts, but it cannot be said to be truly scientific because there is no objective test that could be devised to show it to be false.

Freud's conclusions can be supported, many of them cannot be dismissed and his views have revolutionized man's view of himself.

The Scientific Status of Psychology

Karl Popper had been interested in psychoanalysis but came to realize that its claims to scientific status were insupportable. He formulated a theory of the scientific method but also published his own ideas about the mind which, unlike materialistic ones, did not fully equate with the anatomy and functioning of the brain. He viewed the mind as a repository of subjective experiences, rather than as a bundle of reflexes and brain processes. Popper made the critical distinction between the material world, called "World 1," and the subjective world, called "World 2."

He used this distinction to argue that the thought processes of the human mind do not necessarily depend on the outside world. For instance, the human mind created the sequence of numbers to describe the fact that there are several things which are alike and which can be counted. However, once such abstract sequences are created, they exist autonomously — that is, not separately from circumstances in the material world.

Examples of such autonomous abstractions are the classification of odd versus even numbers, of prime numbers, or similar categories of numbers. These abstractions originate in the human mind (subjective world "World 2"), although they can subsequently be applied to the outside world. They demonstrate the independence of the subjective world from the material world.

But Popper does not stop there. He emphasizes that the human mind actually acts on and modifies material conditions — rather than being passively manipulated by them. For example, as a result of human planning, some city environments have been almost totally created by humans. In other

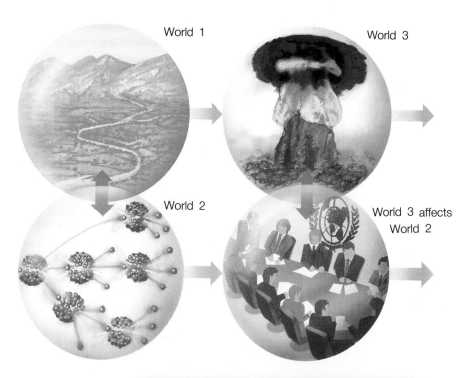

According to Karl Popper, the natural world and the world of the human mind constantly interact and affect each other. Popper calls these worlds World 1 and World 2, respectively, and the product of their interaction — the natural world as changed by the human mind — he calls World 3. Mathematics (bottom) and the theories of nuclear physics belong to World 1, but from them nuclear weapons were developed. These have affected the natural world, if only in terms of increased radiation. This changed world in turn affects the way people think about a whole range of issues. In Popper's terms, World 3 affects World 2.

World 1

World 3

World 2

World 3 affects World 2

words, World 1 is changed by its interaction with World 2. Popper calls this altered material world "World 3." Its existence exemplifies the principle that much of the human mind, which arises from experiences of the world around us, is ultimately determined by the human mind — either our own or others. In this way, using a more modern approach, Popper reasserts the superiority of the mind over matter which the ancient Greeks described — albeit in different terms.

Abnormalities of the Mind

Just as medicine has profited from investigating disease and physical injury, ideas and knowledge of the mind have throughout history been heavily influenced by the study of the abnormal mind. Hippocrates was one of the pioneers of psychiatry, along with other fields of medicine. He was the first to describe epilepsy and the unusual psychological states that sometimes go with it, and to link the mind with the brain.

It was not until the nineteenth century, however, with the gradual accumulation of mentally ill people in asylums, that the study of mental abnormalities really began in earnest. In the asylums were all those who were unable to take care of themselves, or who were a nuisance or danger to others. Vast hospitals were built to house the insane and the feeble-minded, and they are only today beginning to be dismantled as a result of the new-found abilities to treat such complaints and the new attitudes toward mental illness.

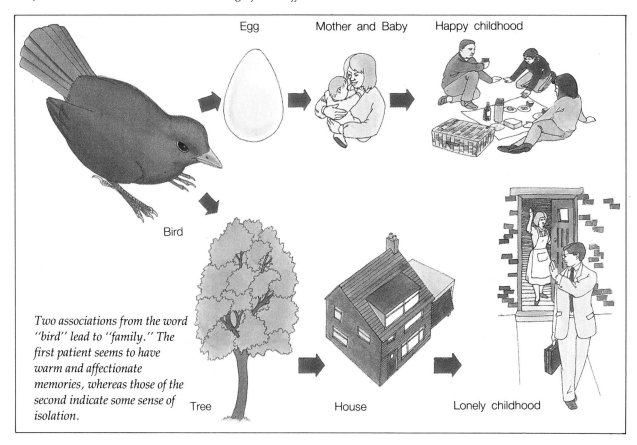

Egg   Mother and Baby   Happy childhood

Bird

Two associations from the word "bird" lead to "family." The first patient seems to have warm and affectionate memories, whereas those of the second indicate some sense of isolation.

Tree   House   Lonely childhood

Studies of patients with mental illnesses made it clear that the various faculties of the mind did not all deteriorate together and to an equal extent. In some conditions concentration and logical thinking were affected, although memory and other intellectual functions were fully preserved. Often this deterioration in concentration and self-control was accompanied by changes in perception, such as hallucinations, and with bizarre and incorrect beliefs, called delusions. This collection of symptoms was first called dementia praecox, and later schizophrenia. When the brains of patients with this condition were examined after death, no obvious abnormalities were found, in contrast with the kinds of conditions in which memory was affected (such as tertiary syphilis or senile dementia). More recently, however, subtle abnormalities have been found in the brains of patients with schizophrenia, and physicians now believe that it is partly a biochemical disorder.

Another important group of conditions first observed in the asylums of the nineteenth century were those in which the emotions or moods were most affected. In such illnesses the most obvious problem was profound depression or elation, in extremes sufficient sometimes to endanger life. Mood could swing back and forth with extraordinary ferocity and rapidity, without apparent cause; such obviously abnormal behavior became known as manic depression.

A group of conditions germane to the development of psychology were the hysterical neuroses. In these the patient has physical symptoms such as paralysis or anesthesia without a physical cause. The great French neurologist Jean Charcot (1825–1893) was an expert in treating these cases, and doctors from throughout the world flocked to Paris to observe his hypnotic techniques. He would hypnotize wheelchair-bound patients and suggest to them that their paralysis would disappear; subsequently, the patient would come to and dramatically get out of the chair and walk away.

Psychoanalytic Therapy

The dramatic demonstrations of Charcot led others to use it. Adherents included the young Austrian Doctor Freud, who successfully treated many cases before giving up hypnosis in favor of his own technique of free association. In this method, the patient's elaborations reveal unconscious themes which are related to the cause of his or her symptom, say hysteria. The associations which emerge point the analyst toward a theory of why this patient has developed this particular symptom.

In deciding how the patient's problem had come about, Freud turned to the universal tendency of the human mind to create symbols as a means of expression. In hysteria, he said, the symptom is a symbolic representation of a trauma which the patient has repressed or pushed into the unconscious. While it remains unconscious, the trauma is free to do immense damage by causing these symbolic symptoms. By free association it can again be made conscious and the link between the trauma and the symptom can be made clear. This process formed the basis of therapeutic interpretation, through which the patient "gained insight" into the illness. He maintained that when the patient achieved this, the symptom disappeared. From such experiences he then went on to develop his theories of the structure of the human mind as already described.

Drugs and Physical Therapies

Many doctors, both before and since Freud, pursued physical treatments for their mentally ill patients. At first this meant cold showers, straitjackets and the like. Then gradually, drugs became available to do specific jobs. Sedatives enable disturbed patients to be calmed without restraint and without being locked up. Antidepressants, discovered in the middle of this century, act on depressed people to correct a relative shortage of neurotransmitters in the central nervous system and so raise their mood back to normal. Antipsychotic drugs, which block dopamine receptors in the brain, have been found which counteract delusions and hallucinations. The very fact that

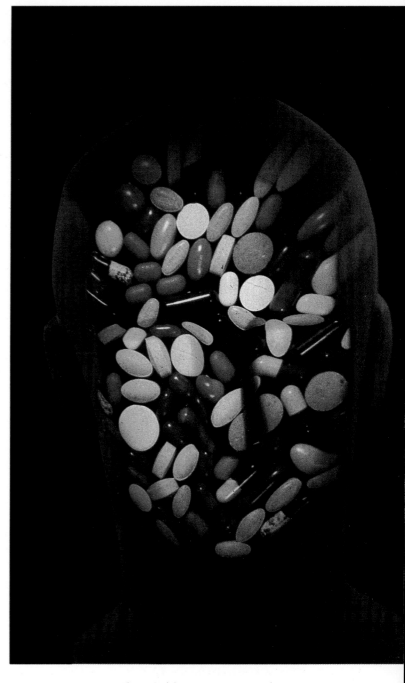

The use of drugs to treat mental disorders was seen as a breakthrough in the early 1950s, and they have helped control and lessen the symptoms of such conditions as schizophrenia, anxiety and depression. With the aid of drugs, many patients who would otherwise require hospitalization have been able to lead relatively normal lives, but medication remains only one element in the physician's armory.

For people to communicate and society to function, signs are essential, and the mind interprets simple symbols immediately. The arrow is probably the simplest; its meaning can be understood by people from almost any culture in the world. Other signs are more complex and specialized — only English-speakers can understand the words in this book, and many scientific and mathematical symbols are understood by only a few people.

drugs can be proved scientifically to have an effect on specific mental disorders is further evidence of the physical reality of the mind and its dependence on processes that take place in the brain and other parts of the body.

Other drugs were also developed which were later found to cause some of the symptoms of mental disorders. Amphetamines made people "high" or "speedy," and their abuse can lead to paranoid psychoses which mimic paranoid schizophrenia. Other drugs made people depressed. In the 1950s and 1960s, several psychedelic drugs became popular, such as LSD and mescaline. These caused distortions of perception, sometimes amounting to hallucinations.

At the same time as drugs were being shown to be effective in treating mental disorders, some doctors were developing an approach to mental problems which rejected the medical model of psychiatry. The Scotsman R. D. Laing (1927–) held that psychoses such as schizophrenia were not illnesses but expressions which it was necessary for sufferers to experience in order to comfort and resolve them. Thus he directly blamed the family for a child's illness. He maintained that a cure was achieved by a corrective therapeutic relationship conducted within a protected environment, rather than by the drugs of a psychiatrist. There the mentally ill would work through their conflicts — indeed, the psychosis itself was part of that process.

Although Laing's methods are thought-provoking, they must be regarded with skepticism. They did not prove to be effective in the treatment of schizophrenia. Further, the indictment of parents was eventually thought to be excessively harsh and simplistic, for there was no real evidence pointing to their culpability, although more recently it has been demonstrated that high expressed emotion (particularly hostility and criticism) by parents of schizophrenics can worsen symptoms in their children.

Ideas and Words

Much of human thought is expressed subjectively in the form of words and images. This split between words and pictures corresponds closely with the statistical analysis of human abilities and

with the very structure and function of the two sides, or hemispheres, of the brain. In general, language abilities are associated with the left hemisphere, visuospatial abilities with the right.

The relationship between thought and language is a central issue in psychology. Of course, our thoughts are really patterns of nervous activity in the brain. Do we really think in words, or are our thoughts something else, neither words nor pictures? How do ideas relate to words and how are they translated into words? How do you know what is meant by the pattern of graphic symbols on the pages of this book?

For a behaviorist this is not a problem. Words are responses, albeit symbolic ones, and although complex need no extra explanation. In the case of a long written work of complex philosophy, the reasons for writing it might be nicely explained by behaviorist logic (the writer is rewarded by status or money), but they cannot enlighten us as to the actual process of transferring ideas into words. Yet this is one of the most important tasks of the human mind and cannot be ignored.

The development of language has been the central focus of the work of the American scholar Noam Chomsky (1928–   ), who is a psycholinguist, philosopher and politician. He argues that there are different basic stages of language development. At birth, the infant brain is already programmed with universal rules which govern the organization and comprehension of sentences from words. Chomsky calls these innate rules "generative transformational grammar." After birth, the child's opportunities for learning in his or her environment, naturally, influence the degree to which individual native ability is developed. These theories transformed linguistics over very few years into an innovative and overarching field that embraces psychology as well as linguistics, and aims at explaining the very nature of communication.

Scientific knowledge of language and thinking, or cognition, has also dramatically improved with the development of the new tools of the twentieth century with which it could be investigated. In particular, the advent of the computer has raised provocative theoretical questions. Today's computers are so powerful that psychologists are serious-

An electroencephalogram (EEG) measures the electrical activity of the brain. The wave patterns recorded change with different levels of consciousness. Fully alert, eight to thirteen irregular waves are seen each second. This rate decreases as the person falls asleep. In deep sleep, one to two large, slow waves occur per second. In dreaming sleep, the EEG waves are similar to those of wakefulness.

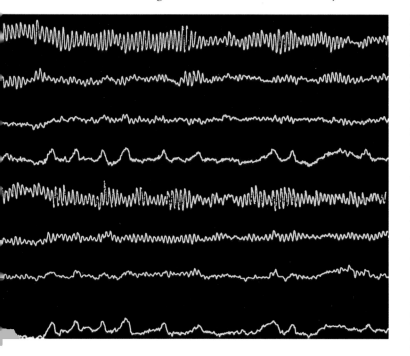

ly asking the question whether or not computers can think. Would a thinking computer have a mind? Can a computer be made to simulate a knowledge of itself as a separate being, in the same way that human beings can experience themselves as individual entities?

Sleep and Consciousness

Freud wrote about the importance of the subconscious and unconscious in determining behavior. How does Freud's idea of the unconscious relate to this word's everyday meaning — for instance, someone who has just been knocked out in a traffic accident? In that situation the brain is "switched off" except for the lower parts which control breathing and other vital functions. In fact, sleep is more akin to the state described by Freud as the unconscious. Indeed Freud called dreams the "Royal Road to the Unconscious" because he thought that their interpretation could lead to important insights into a person's unconscious wishes or conflicts. His views, expounded in his first and perhaps most revolutionary book, *The Interpretation of Dreams*, transformed the thinking world's view of dreaming.

It is now known that during the night we are far from being mentally inactive. When an electroencephalogram (EEG, a recording of brainwaves) is taken throughout the night, several different patterns of sleep can be identified. There are two basic types. The first is called slow-wave sleep, because there are large, slow undulations of the EEG trace during this time, showing that the brain is in a relatively quiescent state. If someone is woken during this time and asked what they were thinking about, they usually report ordinary thoughts, such as what they ate for lunch. During this time the switch mechanism in the brain (the cortex) which connects "intentions to act" with the body muscles which do the acting remains on, so that the sleeper may move a lot, but the brain is quiescent. Sleep-walking occurs in slow-wave sleep in some people.

The second type of sleep, sometimes called paradoxical sleep, would probably have fascinated Freud. The EEG becomes very active and looks almost like the trace obtained during wakefulness. The eyes move rapidly, leading to the name rapid eye movement (REM) sleep. On the other hand, the rest of the muscles of the body, apart from those essential to life, are cut off by the switch just described. When woken — with difficulty — from this type of sleep people report their most vivid dreams, sometimes with bizarre and fantastic occurrences, sometimes just plain odd. People often find that if they wait a few minutes before trying to make a note of their dreams, they are unable to remember them. The most extreme current biological view of dreams is that they are simply the results of random discharges of electrical energy within the brain.

What is sleep for? If it has no function, it is odd that nature demands we spend so much of our lives asleep. The two kinds of sleep do appear to have different uses. Slow-wave sleep is accompanied by an outpouring of restorative hormones into the body's circulation and is probably necessary for repairing wear and tear done during the day. Patients who sleep more after surgical operations heal their wounds more quickly. (Another instance, perhaps, of mind ruling over matter?) Certainly, people who are deliberately deprived of sleep for more than two or three days soon begin to suffer mental disturbances.

A distant view of bridges spanning a river can be seen through an opening in a building in New York. Or can it? The eyes, and therefore the mind, are deceived; the scene is painted on a blank wall.

Newborn babies sleep for an average of sixteen hours in each twenty-four. This drops rapidly in the first year to ten to twelve hours. Babies exhibit the same types of electrical activity of the brain when sleeping·as adults, *including the REM sleep which is characteristic of dreaming. There is a greater proportion of deep sleep, however, and this usually coincides with an increase in the levels of growth hormones in blood.*

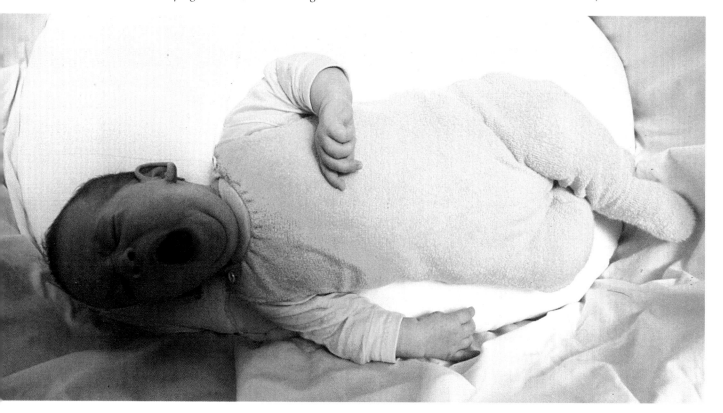

Rapid eye movement sleep is much more difficult to explain. Several scientists have used the fact that dreams are hard to remember, and also that they sometimes seem to consist of previous unwanted memories, to suggest that REM sleep is something to do with programming the brain. The brain may be processing those of the day's occurrences (and those of previous days) which will be entered into the long-term storage banks, and discarding the others. Those which are to be discarded are processed very rapidly and in no particular order so that, when the process is interfered with by waking, the contents of the mind are remembered as bizarre and senseless. Sleep may be nature's way of organizing the filing cabinets of the mind — or perhaps, to use a more modern analogy, of organizing the way that memories are stored away in the mind's computer disks.

Toward a Sleepy Synthesis

The study of sleep shows that the mind can be active in at least three different modes. First there is full wakefulness, the normal conscious condition in which we are aware of the events around us and ready to respond appropriately. Second is slow-wave sleep, in which we are gently processing ordinary sorts of information but can still respond to an external stimulus, such as someone calling our name. Third is REM sleep, in which the contents of the mind are odd and disjointed, and in which it is very difficult to wake up. Nevertheless, some research seems to show that certain external stimuli may "get through" and even be incorporated into dreams, with some somatic effects, during REM sleep.

The study of sleep indicates the value of regarding the mind as both physically associated with brain activity and psychologically related to experience. The interaction between these two views of ourselves is one of the most important areas of knowledge yet to be explored.

"The proper study of mankind is man," wrote Alexander Pope — and there is much to be learned yet.

Carl Jung

Analytical Psychologist

"I am going to say a word. I want you immediately to say another word back to me — whatever comes into your mind on hearing the word I say."

This well-known psychological test, and even game, of associations was devised by Carl Gustav Jung as a means of investigation into the workings of the mind. It was he who also derived the theory of complexes, groups of partly or wholly repressed ideas and associations which can affect a person's behavior.

The son of a Protestant minister, Jung was born in July 1875 at Kesswil, near Basel (Basle) in Switzerland. He grew up to be interested in archeology, yet it was in medicine that he graduated from Zurich University in 1900. He gained his doctorate there two years later, and immediately decided to specialize in psychiatry. It was in Zurich too that he then spent seven years as an assistant in a mental hospital under the direction of the leading expert in schizophrenia, Eugen Bleuler.

It was during this time that Jung formulated his theory of complexes and invented word-association tests. Then in 1907 he met Sigmund Freud, and at once attached himself to him. But his own ideas were

developing, his fame increasing; his lectures on psychiatry at Zurich University were well attended and his book published in 1912 (issued in English in 1916 as *The Psychology of the Unconscious*) was enthusiastically received. So in 1913 he broke with Freud, resigned the presidency of the newly-formed International Psychoanalytical Association, and set up practice on his own.

Twenty years later he was appointed Professor of Psychology at the Zurich Federal Institute of Technology, a post he held until 1941, when he was sixty-six years old. His health then began to deteriorate, although he continued still to practice for another fifteen years. He died at Küsnacht, close to Zurich, in June 1961.

Jung called his techniques analytical psychology in order to distinguish the system from Freud's psychoanalysis. He differed from Freud on three vital points: he distinguished two alternative types of people, introvert and extrovert (terms he invented and popularized); he considered neuroses to result more from immediate problems than from repressed childhood problems (and especially childhood sexual problems); and above all he was certain that survival was a stronger determining factor in libido even than the sexual urge. Infantile sexuality had been one of Freud's central concepts; Jung refuted its importance and derived instead the notion of the collective unconscious — inborn intuitive factors inherited from parents and ancestors, disposing the individual to specific ways of thinking. Elements of such inherited intuitive factors Jung called "archetypes," and by studying peoples of various cultures in America, Africa and India, tried to identify them.

Categorizing people as introverts or extroverts, Jung also derived further classifications for individuals. He theorized that the mind has four essential functions, which he defined as thinking, feeling, sensation and intuition.

Chapter 2

The Developing Mind

Human development, both physical and mental, is determined by a continuous interaction between biological predispositions and the experiences encountered in the course of growing up. Most important are events that occur during the early years of life, because they can have remarkable influence on adult behavior and personality characteristics. To understand the psychological processes of adults — perceptions, patterns of thinking, motives, emotions, conflicts, and ways of coping with conflicts — scientists are attempting to understand how these processes originate and change over time.

The development of the human mind and an understanding of how it works are subjects of universal fascination. One basic assumption underlying the understanding is that our abilities begin in infancy, or even in the womb before birth. This is the basis of developmental psychology. A second assumption is that most new steps in our comprehension of the world depend on the way the previous step was completed, a sequence that has been termed hierarchical integration. If we could move backward through our own individual pasts, we would eventually come to the moment when we were born, or even when we were conceived. One way to understand the human mind is thus to trace its ontological history — that is, its development from embryo and fetus through to adulthood. Another way is to make comparisons of similar behavior between humans and various animal species. This is called comparative psychology.

There are some themes which stand out in connection with the development of the mind of a child. One is represented by the classic controversy about the origin of behavior, the nature versus nurture issue: Is our behavior governed by genetic blueprints or by experience? Although both extremist views have been held through history, an interactionist approach is more tenable today. Our genetic endowment stands ready to be molded by our specific environment. This is demonstrated by the dramatic intellectual improvement of some apparently retarded children after being moved from understimulating institutional settings to more enriched environments.

The essentially social nature of intellect is another important theme in development psychology. A person's genetic endowment and cognitive capacities are geared to forming relationships with other people. The universality of many developmental events is another fundamental theme. A case in point is the ability of all normal six-month-old babies, regardless of culture, to understand that

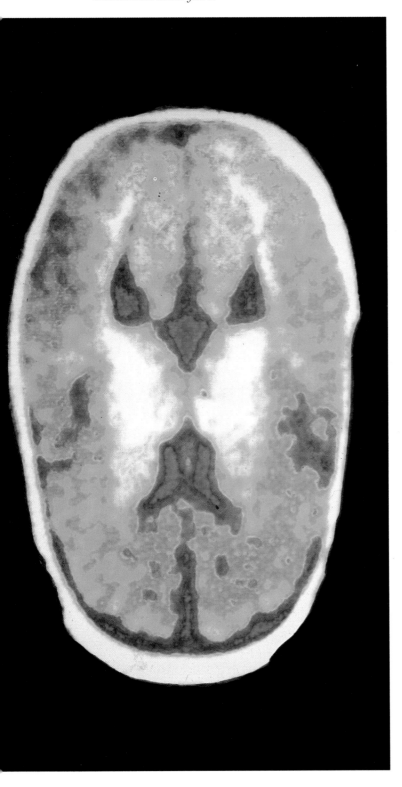

The developing brain of a six-month human infant is represented on a computer scan. The growth of the brain is most rapid during the first three years of life, approaching full size at about seven years.

all objects are permanent fixtures in the world.

The existence of individual differences, alongside of universal developmental psychology, is a fourth theme. For instance what, if anything, differentiates male and female minds? How are such differences embellished by a child's experience?

The Newborn and Infant Periods

For convenience, the term newborn is taken to include the first month of life, and the term infancy the first two years. The seventeenth-century British philosopher John Locke (1632–1704) believed that a baby's mind is blank at birth, a *tabula rasa*. Two hundred years later the American William James argued that human consciousness was always in a constantly active process of perceiving and responding to the world around it. These opposing views form the basis of some current controversies (which will be referred to later) concerning the way in which an infant combines information from many stimulus sources.

Anatomically, all the sensory systems of humans are quite advanced before birth. The maturation of the senses of smell and taste (sixteenth week of gestation) precedes that of hearing (twenty weeks) and vision (twenty-eight weeks). The taste buds, the inner ear and some parts of the eye — the lens, cornea and retina — are fully developed at birth. Other parts of the eye, such as the iris and the front-to-back dimension, grow after birth, as does the outer ear. There is also development of the higher nervous centers which are involved in sensory processing.

The Development of Vision

Research has shown that, even as newborns, we have visual abilities that are well-suited to our needs. Although these abilities are relatively feeble in comparison to adult vision, they develop very rapidly.

The newborn can detect light, dark and color at birth. But focus is relatively poor and slow to adapt to different conditions. It has been suggested that seeing in the newborn is comparable to peripheral vision in adults. Newborns can just see objects at twenty feet which can be seen by adults between 150 and 450 feet distant (different methods of study have given rise to the apparently wide range of these estimates).

At birth the focus is virtually fixed at a distance of about eight inches. This is a typical distance between a mother and her baby when nursing, so this visual characteristic may contribute to the social development of the baby. Despite the blurring of objects outside of this range, the visual capacity of newborns seems biologically adaptive. The ability to focus develops quickly: by four months it improves four to five times. An average child has 20/40 vision by the age of four years, and 20/20 vision is generally achieved by six or seven years of age.

Perception of Depth

Depth perception is important for successfully learning to crawl and walk. There are many clues to depth, including shadows, focusing, coordinating the eyes, and movement in the visual field. In many animals such as kittens, chickens and turtles, this ability is present from birth.

Human babies six months old are aware of changes in depth if placed on a so-called "visual cliff" and persuaded to crawl to their mothers. The "cliff" is actually a transparent box placed over a checkered pattern which drops away steeply on one side, thus giving the impression of depth. By the time the infants can crawl (age six months), they will not cross over to the "deep" end. This same caution is seen in older children who will not swim in deep water. Two-month-old babies also show different responses to depth in visual cliff conditions as measured by their heart rates. But this "depth" discrimination may be a reaction to the different patterns on the deep and shallow sides of the cliff.

Current research is concentrated on delineating the development of specific clues rather than on "depth" as a whole. The clues that have been studied, such as focus, show rapid increases in capacity over the first few months of life.

Recognizing Shapes

As early as the first two weeks, the infant shows the ability to distinguish one stimulus from another, or visual discrimination. Babies appear to use certain strategies in deciding what to look at

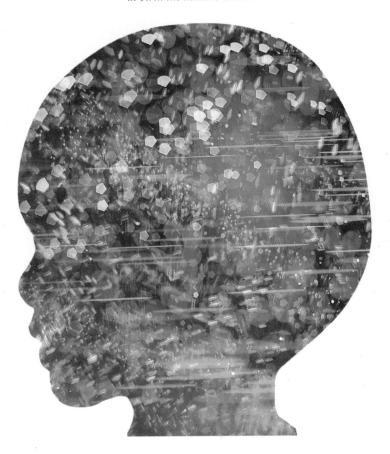

The idea that the mind of a newborn is a "booming, buzzing confusion" was advocated by the psychologist William James. This view opposed that of John Locke, who believed that at birth the mind is blank.

from the choice of elements in their environment. One series of studies showed that newborns are likely to open their eyes widely in a dark room and scan until they detect a contrast between the light levels of two surfaces. When such a contour is discovered, the infant concentrates eye movements on the edge of the shape. Studies of eye movements show that attention to edges continues for about two months, then infants begin to look at certain features of a picture inside its frame. They also exhibit certain preferences — for instance, curved lines are watched more than straight lines, and complex stimuli more than simple ones.

Faces are one exception to the preference for looking at edges shown by very young babies. Even newborns look at features inside the face, not at the extremes. Face-like stimuli are the most looked at; plain surfaces the least. Scrambled faces are viewed less than normal faces, and by four months, infants make different responses toward

A landscape (left) and a face (right) were two pictures used in a test to discover how babies scanned features of their environment. The two pictures were projected as images in front of the children so that their eye movements could be studied using a special mirror arrangement. While the landscape was largely ignored, the image of a face was scanned more thoroughly and for longer periods. Also the younger baby spent most time scanning the edges of the image, whereas the older baby concentrated most attention on the internal details of the face. True recognition of a person does not occur until after the age of six months.

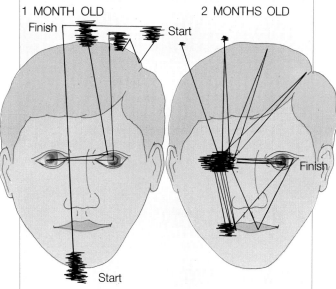

their parents' faces than toward those of strangers. Some psychologists argue that this shows that young infants are social creatures who are strongly attracted to human faces. Others argue that babies are attracted to a certain amount of visual complexity. Whichever explanation is correct, this special treatment of faces is adaptive, causing a baby to be particularly aware of the parents, thus increasing the chances of survival.

Perception of Sounds

The development of hearing is less well understood because of the difficulties involved in determining what a baby hears. A measurement problem is also encountered in clinical settings because detection of impaired hearing is often late; for example, only half of the profoundly deaf children in Europe in 1974 had been identified by the age of three years. Newborn babies respond to changes in loudness with altered body movements or rate of heartbeat. They are not, however, responsive to changes in pitch.

It has been shown that newborns can recognize their mother's voice in the first week. They quicken their rate of sucking when they hear their mother speaking. The same babies do not alter their sucking rates when another woman's voice is heard in the same way.

Babies probably develop the ability to recognize their mothers' voices before birth. Evidence toward this was provided by examining the remarkable correlation of sucking speeds of newborn babies in conjunction with a presentation of a story which had been read aloud by their mothers before birth. The rhythm of the story may, however, by itself have been responsible for this finding. Variations in newborn activity corresponding to the rhythm of a sound are found in several contexts. For instance, a sound which repeats about sixty times a minute often quietens a crying infant. Commercial recordings with such repetitive sounds are marketed to distressed parents who wish to quieten a baby that has failed to respond to other comforts.

The auditory threshold — the loudness required to elicit a response to a particular sound — is high in newborns. The sound intensity required varies from 30 to 70 decibels, depending on the frequency and the technique used. Brainstem responses require 30 decibels over the threshold (the level of loud human speech); behavior changes require 70 decibels (equivalent to the noise level of a motorcycle). Hearing improves gradually over the first few years of life.

Experiments on babies aged between one and eight months show that they can discriminate between almost all the phonetic distinctions that have been tested. For instance, there is renewed vigor in sucking after presenting the sound "pah" to infants following several presentations of "bah." The type of discrimination found in young infants is similar to the categorical perception exhibited by adults, and has adaptive significance for later communication.

There is thus evidence for quite advanced perceptual processing for sounds in infants. Hearing is relatively crude at birth, but improves with age. The discriminatory capacity of infants is, however, quite advanced from an early age, and includes a response to rhythms, to loudness, to some features of the mother's voice, and to linguistically relevant dimensions of speech sounds.

As more effective methods for measuring infant responses are discovered, how the perception of smells, tastes and tactile stimuli develops is also beginning to be charted. The sense of smell, for example, seems to be functional from about four days old.

The facial expressions of babies vary when different tastes are experienced. A relaxed expression occurs when sweet liquid is offered; pursed lips are likely when a sour substance is given; and an opened mouth turned down at the edges is the typical response to a bitter taste. Even in the first few days there is some differentiation of taste.

The newborn baby also has abilities to feel through touching, or tactile abilities. To a limited extent, he or she will withdraw from painful stimuli. The initiation of many of the infant's reflexes in the presence of a tactile stimulus is further evidence of his or her responses to touch. For example, in the walking reflex, slight pressure on the ball of one foot sets off a stepping motion in the other foot.

Senses in Combination

How does the young infant relate sounds to pictures? Smells to tastes? Touch to sight? Such questions about how the mind combines sensory information are at the center of a controversy involving the theory of developmental psychology. Some theorists argue that, as the infant grows, the separate perceptual experiences are integrated. This notion suggests that when babies

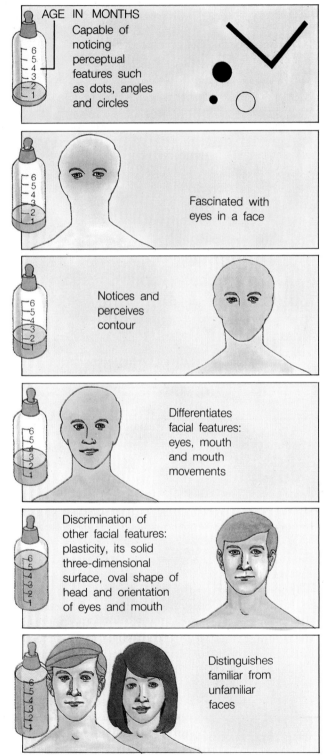

AGE IN MONTHS
Capable of noticing perceptual features such as dots, angles and circles

Fascinated with eyes in a face

Notices and perceives contour

Differentiates facial features: eyes, mouth and mouth movements

Discrimination of other facial features: plasticity, its solid three-dimensional surface, oval shape of head and orientation of eyes and mouth

Distinguishes familiar from unfamiliar faces

reliably turn toward someone speaking behind them at six to seven months of age, they are then capable of making a connection between the sound and the sight of the speaker.

Other theorists take the opposite point of view — that babies learn to differentiate between one sense and the others as they mature. The contention here is that the infant perceives a stimulus as a whole, and is able to distinguish between its components only as he or she matures. That the speaker's voice and image are as one is the fundamental sensory experience, according to this theory.

Evidence of cross perception comes from work with babies born blind. An ultrasound device was fitted to a headset in such a way that the pitch of the sound varied with the distance to an object; and the side of the sound (to left or right ear) depended on the object's location. Blind babies from five to twelve months old learned very quickly (within hours or days) to use the device to accurately reach for objects and to "navigate" in three dimensions. Signs of joy which accompanied its use were said to indicate that these infants

could glean spatial information about the world from auditory clues. A thirteen-month-old baby and an adult who were fitted with the ultrasound transmitters were unable to adjust to it so readily. The older baby kept putting objects to his ear, as if they were the source of the sound. According to the differentiation theory, this demonstrates that sound is treated as a separable modality from about twelve months of age.

Development of Object Concepts

An important aspect of all perception is the development of the concept of an object. This subject was a major concern of Jean Piaget's seminal studies of intellectual development of the child. He argues that, in the first few months of life, the infant does not accurately perceive himself or herself as separate from other things in the world. If infants only a few weeks old are shown an illusory object made by casting a shadow on a screen, they reach out for the object and seem surprised when it is not present. This indicates how basic is the infant's sense of object identity. To understand the world, we must appreciate that

objects have permanence — that is, they exist whether or not we perceive them directly. We must also understand they they have constant properties from one encounter to the next — for example that a toy train is the same object before and after it goes through a tunnel. This is called object permanence.

An understanding of object permanence develops over the first twelve months. Up to two months old, the infant seems surprised by the reappearance of a toy train from a tunnel. Anything that is not perceived, does not exist; that is, out of sight is out of mind. Between two and six months, the infant seems surprised if a toy does not reappear if it is covered and then uncovered. Between six and eight months the child not only predicts the existence of an object which has disappeared, he or she also looks over the edge of a crib for it. It is at this age that an infant's eyes move as if to follow the toy train through the tunnel, expecting it to come out at the other end at the same speed; the visual system is predicting constant motion. After eight months, the infant actively searches for an object which is completely

This unhappy baby, far from being amused by the multitude of colorful items in the crib, may be crying because he is unable to respond to such a large amount of stimulation. Although increased stimulation at an early age has been found to accelerate the development of visual and motor skills, it is not effective until infants are sufficiently mature mentally.

0-2

SENSORIMOTOR

Discovers actions have an effect on the environment

Object permanence

2-7

PREOPERATIONAL

Egocentric

Counting

Symbolic actions

Jean Piaget identified four stages of a child's intellectual development. By the age of two a baby has discovered the relationship between sensations and motor behavior, and has learned that objects continue to exist even though they are no longer visible. During the preoperational stage, the child begins to use language and represent actions symbolically, but is still egocentric, having difficulty in taking the viewpoint of others. The child becomes capable of logical thought during the concrete operational stage, achieves conservation concepts and is able to order objects along a dimension. By twelve years old, the child should be able to think in abstract terms, isolating elements of a problem and exploring all possible solutions.

hidden in new places by removing a cover. Significantly, perhaps, the attachment between an infant and the mother is also fully-fledged at six months, when the understanding of object permanence appears.

In general, research on the various modes of perception suggests that they are probably highly interdependent in the development of the infant. This survey of the perceptual capacities in infancy has indicated that, despite relative immaturity, even the newborn is capable of actively adapting to his or her environment. Every baby possesses the necessary apparatus for survival, including social behavior and crude mental organization of the many events in the environment.

Early Response Capabilities

There are many reasons for scientists to study the physical development of an infant when they are interested in the mind of the child. One is that

7-12

CONCRETE OPERATIONAL

Mass, weight and number conservation

Ordering

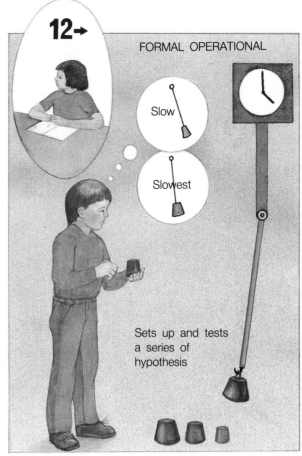

12→

FORMAL OPERATIONAL

Slow

Slowest

Sets up and tests a series of hypothesis

physical growth enables an infant to make new responses. Each new response may in turn affect the way the baby is treated by others.

Crying is an example of this. Initially, the crying is a reflex action, important in taking the first breath. A baby's cry gets higher in pitch during the first month as the movements of the vocal cords become better coordinated. By four weeks, the cords close simultaneously more often than in the first few days of life, increasing the cry's pitch.

The cry also has a survival function; it makes adults pay attention to the infant. Many adults can recognize different sorts of crying — for example, a hunger cry can be differentiated from a pain cry. Some mothers are able to identify the cry of their own infants after 48 hours despite the scientifically measured fact that newborns on average cry only about seven per cent of the time.

As a baby grows, the cry changes — through more refined motor control of the articulatory apparatus — to the more common vocalizations, babbling and cooing. By one year old, the cry is used to evoke and maintain the attention of an adult. The baby cries more in an adult's arms at this age, in contrast to the soothing effect of being cradled in the arms in the newborn period.

Motor growth plays a major role in the experience a baby acquires. When a child is able to crawl, a new world is opened up for exploration. This growth roughly follows certain sequences that serve the changing needs of the developing human being. One trend is for maturation to proceed from head to toe: the ability to control the head and neck occurs earlier in the first year than the ability to use the lower limbs. This is called cephalocaudal development.

Another trend is for maturation to proceed from the center of the body to the periphery. Thus, in reaching for objects, the infant is first able to use his or her arms to make so-called gross motor

41

A loud cry and a firm grip are two of the first observable responses made by a neonate. From the moment of birth, newborns explore their environment through their senses and respond by means of reflexes.

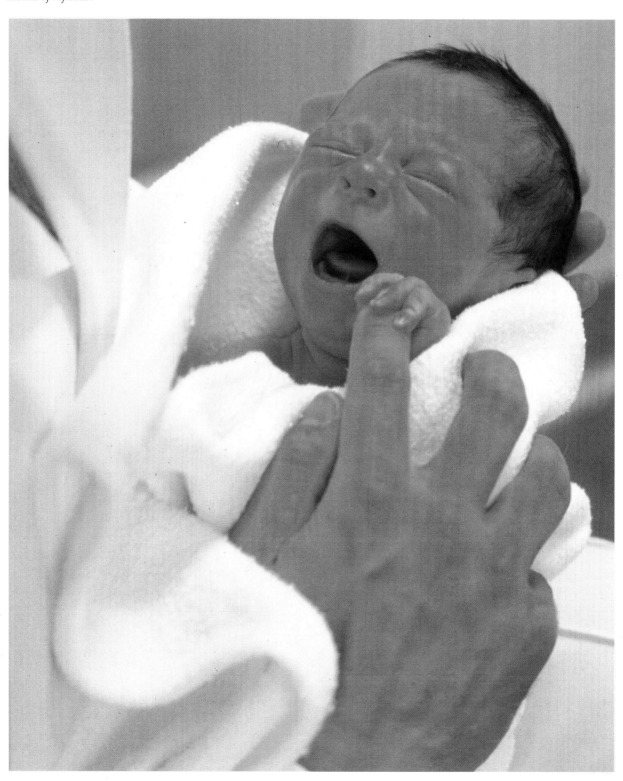

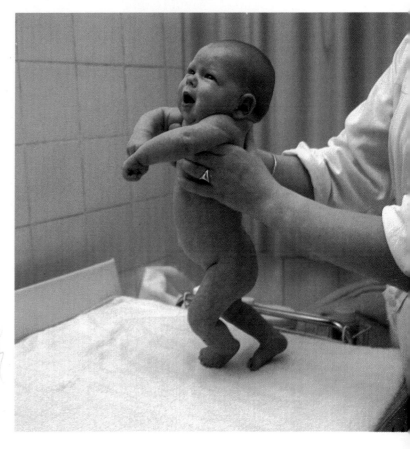

At about six weeks old, a baby held upright makes walking movements. This reflex action disappears for nearly a year until, as a result of neuromuscular maturation, the baby consciously attempts to walk.

movements, before fine motor movements of the hand, at the periphery of the body. This is called proximodistal development.

The acquisition of individual skills also follows a fairly consistent pattern. Initially, the newborn demonstrates crude, innate, automatic movements, or reflexes — such as the baby's walking reflex at birth. Later, these automatic movements cease; at two to three months, walking can no longer be elicited. Later still, the skill returns in a mature form under voluntary control. Although repeated practice of mature skills may be extremely beneficial, very early training, before the skills have been attained, is ultimately only marginally helpful.

The role motor development plays in the mental life of a child is emphasized in the theory of intellectual development proposed by Jean Piaget. He argues that all thought arises from action. He sees the child as an active participant in the growth process, building up lawful expectations, or schemas, about the world. To Piaget, intelligence is an adaptive biological process which begins with sensorimotor experience. As new response capabilities develop, the child's ability to impose mental organization or structure on events in the outside world advances. This increasing ability is called "assimilation."

For instance, Piaget's theory may be illustrated by the development of play behavior during infancy. Initially the baby plays mostly with his or her limbs and explores the body. By about six months single objects are played with; then multiple objects become the focus of an infant's interest. At the end of the second year, the child begins to use symbolic play, pretending to make a cup of coffee for example, or using a block to represent a truck. Piaget argues that the development of play illustrates the way that thought has been molded by action inasmuch as maturation gradually provides the opportunity for more and more abstract thinking.

In these ways physical maturation is important in mental development. It enables a child to accommodate to the environment by bringing him or her into contact with new objects. Through this contact, growth, in turn, influences interrelations with others in the infant's world. Interaction between physical capability, mental development and social abilities is an apt description of the first two years of life.

Early Socialization

Babies adapt to some features of the adult world after a few months. For instance, newborns sleep about seventy to eighty per cent of each twenty-four hours. The times at which they are awake follow a sequence which involves about seven or eight naps a day. By the age of one year, they sleep, on average, only fifty per cent of the time, and take only two or three daytime naps. Most babies sleep right through the night by 28 weeks — usually to the relief of tired parents.

Requirements for feeding change similarly in the first year: from six to eight feeds a day at birth to three or four meals daily at one year. These adaptations arise partly from physical development, but they may also represent the infant's response

*Within sight of their mothers, a
group of toddlers discover new toys.
Although happy in the company of
their peers, babies less than two years
old usually prefer to play
independently alongside each other
rather than cooperatively. They are
not yet ready to share, and may
vigorously defend what they regard
as their own property.*

to the situation provided by his or her caretakers.

The infant is also a participant in many cycles of mutual action and reaction during the first two years. In these, a baby's behavior sets off a response in an adult, which in turn elicits more activity in the infant, and so on.

Such action-and-reaction cycles are the earliest form of social interaction in the infant's life. Even in the first few days of life, there is a mutual cycle during feeding. An adult gently jiggles a baby when he or she pauses between bursts of sucking. The duration and timing of the jiggles by the adult are intended to elicit the optimal response from the infant.

More mature instances of action and reaction occur when the infant and parent exchange smiles (two to six months) or vocalizations (five months onward). The parent and baby each seem to time their actions to elicit an optimal response from the other. For example, they wait for a short time after

the smile of the other. This is when attention is still on the prior exchange and another smile is likely to be elicited.

The selective responsiveness of even a three-month-old baby may be taken as evidence of these cycles. He or she does not smile at profiles of adult heads or when the adult stares with a poker face. Babies require face-to-face contact to play their part. Some child psychologists, psychiatrists and pediatricians, such as Daniel Stern and T. Berry Brazetton, argue that the adult and infant form an interacting system in which these are shared goals and shared development.

Relationships With Others

During the infancy period, babies begin to show attachment to one other person (or sometimes a few people). Between eight and twelve months old, babies exhibit "stranger anxiety" in response to unfamiliar adults. The presence of an "attachment figure" allays this distress. The fact that babies exhibit both of these tendencies indicates that they can recognize and discriminate their attachment figure(s) from the rest of the world.

A related phenomenon, "separation anxiety," occurs between ten months and two years, when infants cry and show other signs of distress when an attachment figure leaves their presence. The severity of separation anxiety varies with cultural child-rearing practices and the quality of parenting. In some African countries, where infants are nursed until they are two years old, separation anxiety is especially intense compared to that found in American babies, who are more likely to have experienced periods of separation from parents. This capacity to differentiate familiar and unfamiliar people also generalizes to the infant's response to his or her environment, so that new places may evoke similar distress.

During infancy, interactions with other people, and with varied stimulation, are crucial for later social adjustment. Lack of opportunity to form attachments at this stage may cause young children to be unable to form typical peer relationships or to explore their environment normally. Such deficient development has been seen in children raised in institutions where little contact with adults occurs, and is called "hospitalism" by the

Almost all boys in Burma are expected to join a monastery for a period of training as novice monks. Boys may make this departure into an organized, disciplined life at as young as six years old.

Austrian psychiatrist René Spitz. Fortunately, enhanced social stimulation can usually overcome the initial difficulties encountered by those who have been so deprived early in life. More attention is also being paid to stimulating infants in institutional settings, such as special babycare units in hospitals.

An Evolutionary View of Development

Before considering the characteristics of the developing mind after infancy, it is worthwhile to consider human development from an evolutionary perspective. There are many branches of a complete developmental history of species, or phylogeny, and within each branch biological structures range from "less evolved" to "more evolved." Species themselves range from primitive to advanced.

The "imprinting" phenomenon provides a helpful illustration. Imprinting occurs when a chosen object of attachment is determined during a short, critical period of infancy. This type of relationship formation occurs in some birds, on one branch of the phylogenic tree, and in primates, on another branch. Ethologists, animal behaviorists who focus on evolutionary issues, have demonstrated imprinting in precocial birds, which are birds that hatch with a covering of fine feathers, or down. They imprint on any object or person which is mobile almost immediately after hatching.

A hatchling duck will imprint on, and follow, almost any animal or object that is seen in the critical period immediately after hatching. In some early studies, the experimenters themselves became the attachment object for young birds. When the scientist who was the imprinted object was present, there was less distress exhibited by the young in normally threatening situations. Ethologists argue that this strong, rapid attachment is adaptive, because the first object seen after hatching is typically a parent. Staying near the parent during infancy usually promotes species survival, because protection is then available at the time during which the young is dependent on its parents for survival.

In one primate species, the rhesus monkey, attachment is also formed in an early "critical period." This early attachment is important for the

later social adaptation of the animal. An infant monkey denied physical contact with a warm, soft object in the first six weeks of life exhibited increased separation anxiety in comparison with one reared normally, and as a young adult it tended to be withdrawn and failed to take an active role in the monkey hierarchy.

Attachment in humans is a similar example of parallel evolutionary development inasmuch as humans occupy another branch of the primate order from monkeys. Thus, it may be said that the existence of attitudes of behavior in three phylogenic branches argues that it is generally adaptive in social species.

However, there are also differences in the nature of attachment on each of the branches. For instance, human attachment occurs later than attachment in birds. In human beings, as long as there are repeated encounters with one or more other people, social adjustment in later life is likely to be adequate. In birds, the relatively short critical period is followed by specific bonding.

The evolutionary perspective permits the development of behavior to be traced between advancing species or members of a species. Mutual interactions in human beings is an excellent example. This behavior, which requires feedback adjustment from both parent and child, probably represents an evolutionary advancement over that of less highly evolved animals. Some theorists argue that the "teaching role," such as smiling at the infant at an optimal time to elicit further interaction, is one way in which humans are unique. Eventually, this behavior is elaborated into the teacher-student or even superior-worker relationships, in which there are deliberate, long-term efforts to teach.

Instances of such carefully timed interactions are seen only rarely in non-human species. For example, whales use mutual feedback when the young

Smiling and cooing, this two-month infant enjoys a sociable rapport with his mother. By vocalizing and smiling in return, and carefully timing her own responses, the mother stimulates an even more enthusiastic response from her baby.

learn to swim soon after birth. Pushing the infant to the surface to breathe, and modeling by the parent, occurs for only a short time, and then this mutually interactive behavior ceases.

A consideration of the development of other species allows a better understanding of human development. While there are some major similarities among the behaviors of different species, there are also considerable differences. Given that scientists believe that there are no accidents in evolution, this perspective gives an insight into human adaptation.

Moral reasoning also proceeds in stages that appear closely related to the stages of cognitive development. Children under the age of seven tend to be absolute in their moral judgments, evaluating actions in terms of their consequences without regard to the circumstances. At later stages they evaluate actions in terms of conventional rules and norms as laid down by the society in which they are reared. Only a minority progress to the highest levels of moral reasoning, in which moral judgments are based on complex considerations, including intention, attenuating circumstances, social contracts and democratic law, and universal principles of ethics and justice.

As a generalization, it seems that the higher the level of moral reasoning a child manifests, the more likely he or she is to behave morally. The relationship does not exist in a vacuum. Moral behavior, like other behavior is influenced through the observation and imitation of models, through the verbalization — by others — of moral rules and prohibitions, and through rewards for conforming to social rules and punishment for transgressions.

Research has shown that parents who are warm and loving, and who rely on inductive discipline — providing explanations or reasons for requiring a change of behavior in the child and stressing in particular the needs and emotions of others — have children who show the highest levels of moral maturity. On the other hand, children who are deprived of the opportunity to form attachment bonds early in life may grow into "affectionless characters" unable to keep rules and failing to show guilt for transgressions.

Pro-social behaviors or positive social behaviors

such as generosity, caring and helping are also influenced by exposure to pro-social models and cultural background, as well as the child's level of development. Mexican-American children, for example, are generally brought up in an environment that trains them to be more cooperative and less competitive than are contemporary Caucasian-American children.

Aggressive and antisocial behavior are also influenced by social factors, but there is evidence of a biological basis for them. Data from animal studies support the concept of genetic contribution to individual differences in aggression. Further evidence of the stability of aggressive tendencies across time and situation is consistent with this conclusion.

Certain aggressive responses, such as clenching the teeth, making fists and stamping the feet, appear to be innately "wired into" the neuro-muscular system because children born blind and deaf display these behaviors even though they have never had the opportunity to observe them. Damage to certain parts of the brain may also influence levels of aggression.

On the other hand, a biological theory of aggression must take into account the likelihood of a complex interaction between biological and social causation. There is abundant evidence that aggression can be strongly influenced by social and environmental factors, including cultural attitudes and expectations, exposure to aggressive models, and child-rearing practices. A history of rejection and frustration from family or peer groups, overly harsh or inconsistent discipline or permissiveness from authoritarian figures, and reinforcement for aggressive behavior are all associated with high levels of aggression.

There has been much concern that exposure to media violence might increase aggression by teaching new aggressive behaviors, disinhibiting aggressive responses, providing aggressive cues and altering value systems by encouraging acceptance of violence, and distorting views about conflict resolution. Although some studies overwhelmingly support this view, the issues are clearly complex, and further research is needed to throw light on the conditions under which media violence is most and least likely to facilitate ag-

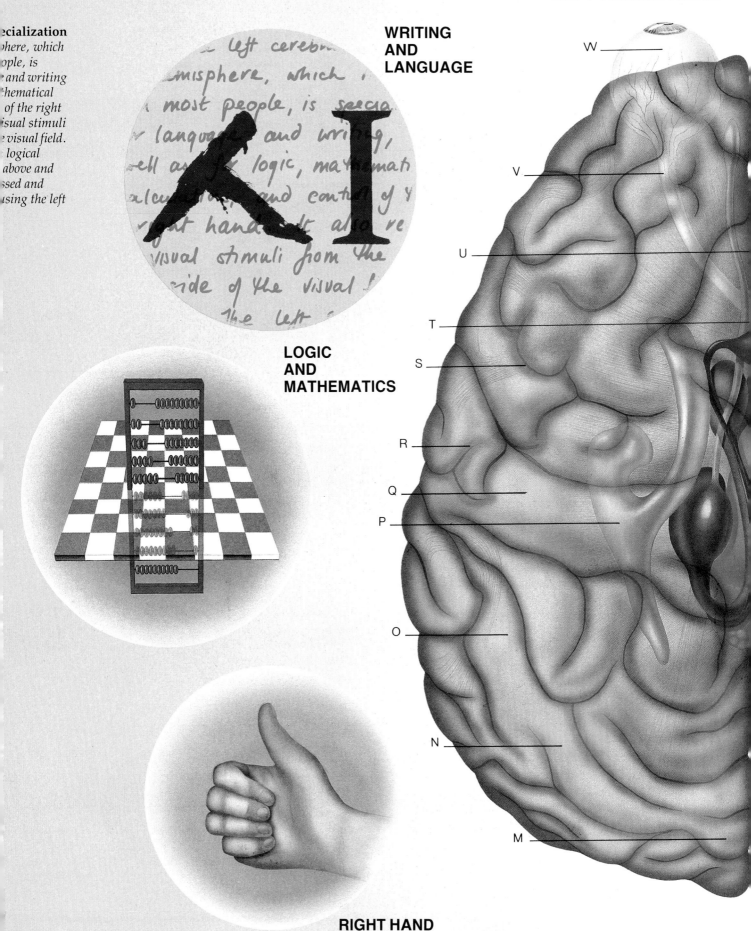

ecialization
phere, which
ople, is
e and writing
thematical
of the right
isual stimuli
e visual field.
logical
above and
ssed and
using the left

**WRITING
AND
LANGUAGE**

**LOGIC
AND
MATHEMATICS**

RIGHT HAND

W _____

V _____

U _____

T _____

S _____

R _____

Q _____

P _____

O _____

N _____

M _____

The brain shows considerable specialization within its structure. The most obvious feature is the division of the cerebrum into two parts, called the cerebral hemispheres. These are linked by bundles of nerve fibers, which join the hemispheres at the corpus callosum and form other vital connections elsewhere in the brain. Despite these links, however, research shows that there are differences between the hemispheres' functions and that each tends to specialize in different fields.

The central illustration shows some of the main structures of the brain, viewed from above. These include the olfactory bulb(A) and tract(B), pituitary gland(C), anterior commissure(D), mammillary body(E), hypothalamus(F), thalamus(G), stria terminalis(H), amygdala(I), hippocampus(J), fornix(K) and choroid plexus(L), which are structurally associated with, or form part of, the limbic system, and are concerned with many aspects of emotion, memory, pleasure, aggression and other features of behavior. Close to these are the brain's ventricles(P), essential reservoirs of cerebrospinal fluid. Connecting the two hemispheres are the fibers of the corpus callosum(U). The optic nerves(V) from the eyes(W) cross at the optic chiasma(T) before leading to the two primary visual areas(M) at the back of the cerebrum. Less clearly defined are areas of the cerebral cortex that are associated with the perception of written or spoken language and sound. These areas include the primary visual(M) and auditory(R) areas; both link with Wernicke's area(O), either by way of the angular gyrus(N) or directly. Impulses pass from there through the arcuate fasciculus(Q) to Broca's area(S), which initiates the appropriate motor response.

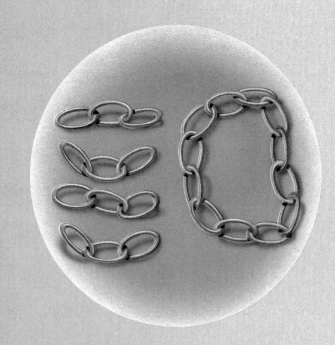

Puzzle 1
How can four short chains (above) be joined together to form a circular chain by opening and closing only three links?

Puzzle 2
How can four straight lines be made to pass through all nine balls (below) so that the second, third and fourth lines all continue from the points at which the previous line finished?

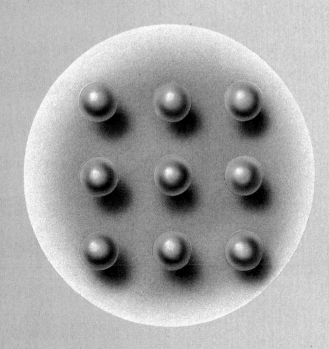

Left hemispheric sp
The left cerebral hemis
is dominant in most pe
specialized for languag
as well as for logic, ma
calculation and contro
hand. It also receives v
from the right side of th
Problems that require
solution, such as those
below, tend to be proce
solved predominantly
cerebral hemisphere.

Like the troops of opposing armies, ranks of ornate chessmen face each other ready to do battle. A product of the human mind, the game of chess and its forerunners have provided people with intellectual exercise for nearly two thousand years.

*al hemisphere tends
ion-verbal skills, like
art and music, or
ree-dimensional
e. It also controls the
ceives visual stimuli
le of the visual field.
are more visual than
those above and
be processed and
nantly using the
emisphere.*

Puzzle 3
*Some of the letters (above) are
rotated and some are back-to-front;
they also form a simple pattern with
one false element. Which is it?*

Puzzle 4
*An ant takes from sunrise to sunset
to climb up a long spiral path
(below), and the same time next
day to walk down again. Is there one
place the ant will be at the same time
of day on both-trips?*

Key to central illustration
A. Olfactory bulb
B. Olfactory tract
C. Pituitary gland
D. Anterior commissure
E. Mammillary body
F. Hypothalamus
G. Thalamus
H. Stria terminalis
I. Amygdala
J. Hippocampus
K. Fornix
L. Choroid plexus
M. Primary visual area
N. Angular gyrus
O. Wernicke's area
P. Ventricle
Q. Arcuate fasciculus
R. Primary auditory area
S. Broca's area
T. Optic chiasma
U. Corpus callosum
V. Optic nerve
W. Eye

Answers
Puzzle 1
*The easiest way to join the chains is
to open all three links of one short
chain and use these to join all the
others together.*

Puzzle 2
*Four consecutive lines can connect
the nine balls if the first line is a
diagonal, joining two corners and
the central ball, and the other three
extend to points beyond the limits of
the square and pass through two
balls in the middle of two adjacent
sides.*

Puzzle 3
*The odd one out is the third down on
the right, which is oriented normally
although rotated, whereas the others
on the right are mirror images.*

Puzzle 4
*To prove that there must be one
point occupied at the same time of
day, imagine the two journeys
superimposed, or two ants starting
from bottom and top
simultaneously: the point where
they meet must be the one common
to both journeys.*

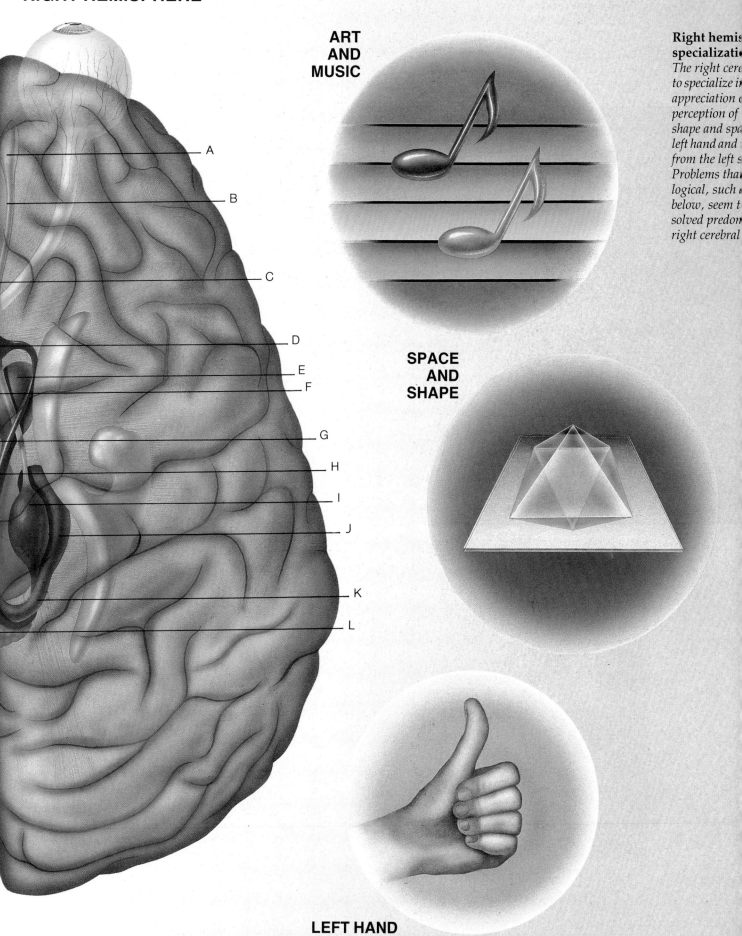

RIGHT HEMISPHERE

A
B
C
D
E
F
G
H
I
J
K
L

ART AND MUSIC

SPACE AND SHAPE

LEFT HAND

Right hemis **specializati**
The right cere
to specialize i
appreciation
perception of
shape and spa
left hand and
from the left s
Problems tha
logical, such
below, seem t
solved predom
right cerebral

Scientists have pointed out the similarity between aggressive behaviors in animals (below) *and humans* (bottom). *They suggest that all humans have inherited innate tendencies to behave aggressively.*

gression, and the differential effects on different individuals of viewing violence.

Personality and Social Development

There is no generally agreed definition of personality. Broadly speaking, it is a term that has traditionally been used by psychologists to refer to the enduring, relatively stable characteristics of an individual which determine his or her unique means of adapting and relating to the environment. Thus, personality theorists concern themselves with describing and explaining individual differences between people in their manner of thinking, feeling and behaving.

The existence of relatively stable personality traits has been seriously called into question. Noting that people often show remarkably little consistency in their behavior over time and across situations, some theorists have argued that behavior is determined by stimulus conditions and is "situation-specific." Often cited in support of this view is a study of children placed in situations in which they were given the opportunity to lie, cheat and steal money, apparently without risk of detection. The results showed that few manifested a consistent trait of honesty across these different situations.

Similarly, it has been found that people tend to explain their own behavior in terms of situational factors, whereas they tend to rely on trait, or dispositional, explanations when making judgments on the behavior of others. One reason for this is that people are more aware of inconsistencies in their own behavior than in that of others; they can recall having behaved differently in the past. These findings argue against the existence of stable personality traits.

There is, however, evidence for the consistency over time of at least some traits — among them aggression, sociability and consistency. It is now generally accepted that behavior is a joint function of the person and the situation. Any behavioral outcome is the result of reciprocal interactions between the person, with his or her unique characteristics, and the situation with its own particular attributes.

An individual's characteristics are the outcome of complex interactions between a great many bio-

logical and environmental/social factors. These include differences in genetic makeup, cultural attitudes and values, parental attitudes and methods of child rearing, and a variety of more or less unique learning experiences. Even such natural factors as the climate — by determining manner of subsistence and settlement patterns — may influence personality development.

There is relatively little evidence for the direct inheritance of personality traits. This is probably due in part to ambiguities in the definition of personality, and in part from the fact that, unlike eye color, for example, personality characteristics tend not to be present in an all-or-nothing fashion. Rather, people can be placed on a continuum with respect to such traits as sociability, apathy, and so on. To the extent that such characteristics are under genetic control, they are most likely determined by a number of interacting genes.

Several lines of evidence suggest a genetic basis for a collection of related temperamental traits, including extroversion, activity, emotionality, sociability and impulsiveness. Selective breeding experiments and studies of animals reared in controlled environments have revealed differences along one or more of these dimensions between breeds of dogs or strains of mice which cannot be ascribed to differences in learning experiences.

At the human level, identical twin pairs have repeatedly been found to correspond more than fraternal pairs on measures of these traits. Longitudinal data of infant temperament also support the existence of enduring personality traits. According to clinicians such as the American psychologist Jerome Kagan and the American psychiatrists Stella Chess and Alexander Thomas, even infants show tendencies toward distinctive personality. Among very young babies, temperamental characteristics that appear to be innate may be early manifestations of later traits. Where-

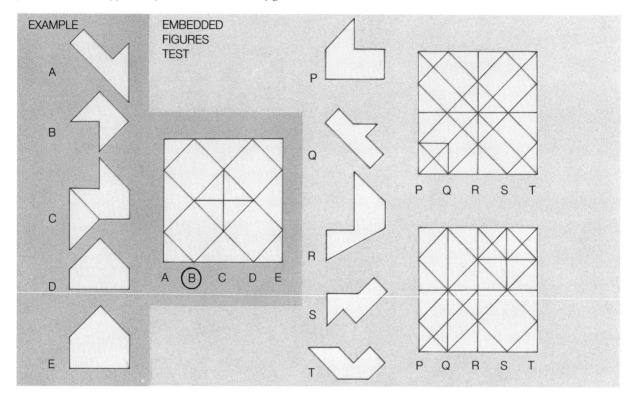

as some infants ("easy" babies) are for the most part happy, adapt readily to new situations, are regular in their routines and moderately responsive to stimulation, others ("difficult" babies) are the opposite. A third group ("slow-to-warm-up" babies) can best be described as "passively resistant" — for example, they let food drool from their mouths rather than swallow it or spit it out. Whether or not these early differences are indeed precursors of personality traits, they are, in any event, likely to influence the nature of the dynamic relationship between mother and child, and in so doing elicit different reactions — which help to shape the developing personality.

Although evidence for the inheritance of personality traits as such is limited, there is compelling support for the relationship between physiological factors and behavior. It is possible that much of what we see as individual differences in behavior may be explained by these factors.

Extremes of biochemical functioning (for example, hyper- and hypothyroidism) can also produce marked behavioral effects. But even within the normal range, there is variation in glandular activity of the order of 300 to 500 per cent, and this could well account for some variations in personality. Such a view is supported by studies of dogs reared in controlled environments in which it has been found that temperamental differences between breeds are related to differences in the sizes of the thyroid and pituitary glands. The clearest example of the relevance of biochemical functioning to personality, and the one most widely documented, concerns the relationship between sex hormones and behavior.

The notion that differences in physiological functioning underlie differences in personality is central to at least one major theory. According to the British psychologist Hans Eysenck introverts are more sensitive to stimulation than are extroverts. They therefore seek to avoid stimulation, preferring quiet solitary pursuits to being with people. Extroverts, on the other hand, being characterized by low levels of cortical arousal, constantly seek stimulation, crave excitement and prefer being with other people to being alone.

Daredevil antics may be considered characteristic of an extrovert, occurring at one end of the introvert-extrovert behavioral dimension upon which Hans Eysenck (bottom) classified personality types.

Notwithstanding the fact that people may change their physical shape and appearance to some extent throughout the course of life — for example, through weight-reducing exercise or plastic surgery — differences between individuals in physique and the appearace generally are, like differences in physiological and biochemical functioning, largely under genetic control. But the view that some gene which predisposes to a particular body type might also predispose to a particular type of temperament appears to be without foundation. There are, however, at least two ways in which body build (and, for that matter, physical handicaps) might conceivably exert an influence on personality development. One is by imposing limits on a child's activities and experiences, and the other is through the reactions of others.

Regarding the second of these possibilities, there is considerable evidence that from the age of about six years onward people hold stereotypes about physique and personality which are favorable to mesomorphs (muscular, athletic types) but unfavorable to endomorphs (short, obese types) and ectomorphs (tall, frail types). In experiments in which people have been asked to assign personality descriptions to silhouettes representing the various body types, the mesomorph is thus commonly described as confident, adventurous, brave, helpful, the one most likely to be chosen as a friend and to make a good leader, doctor, soldier, professor, and so on. The endomorph on the other hand is described as cheerful, but lazy, selfish, self-indulgent and (by very young children) as ugly, dirty, and stupid, one who is always being teased. The ectomorph is described as detached and tense, a worrier.

Similarly, people are willing to attribute to others whom they regard as physically attractive a host of positive characteristics which they do not necessarily possess. They readily endow unattractive individuals with less desirable characteristics (including neurological disorders). Because it is very difficult not to behave as one knows one is expected to behave, such stereotypes can easily become self-fulfilling prophecies. This has been demonstrated in classroom experiments in which attractive children have been found to achieve better grades than their equally intelligent — but

Jerome Bruner

Cognition and Representation

Many psychologists believe that cognition — awareness, the ability to think in terms of both self and the environment — develops in a person from infancy to adulthood following a set path with specific and recognizable stages. Two scientists have successfully claimed to have identified those stages: one is Heinz Werner, whose "dimensions" are a series of opposites; the other is the pioneering American psychologist and educational specialist Jerome Seymour Bruner.

Bruner was born in New York City in October 1915, the son of a watch manufacturer. Educated at Duke University and then Harvard, it was from the latter that he received his doctorate in 1941. For much of World War II, however, he was in France as a member of Army Intelligence. In 1952 he became Professor of Psychology at Harvard, and then Director of the Center for Cognitive Studies, a post he held until 1972. In that year he moved to Oxford University in England, as Watts Professor of Psychology.

The stages in cognitive development identified by Bruner were three; he called them the three modes of representation, suggesting that there are three levels of awareness through which we

all have progressively to pass.

The "enactive" level of the young infant relies on physical action: what a baby *does* is *what* and *how* he or she thinks; at such an age the infant has no other means of expression.

The next stage is the "iconic" level, at around the age of two or three, during which the child replaces physical action with "images" perceived through any of the senses. The child can thus remember with clarity and precision former sensory experiences.

The final stage is the "symbolic" level, in which the sensory images are in turn replaced by verbal expression. To the child from about age five or six, such a mode of expression may be just as

representational, although the use of words naturally increases in scope and power as the vocabulary enlarges with learning, as does also the habituation to the transformational rules of grammar and syntax. It may in fact take many years before sufficient command of expression is acquired to be able to fully represent every nuance of meaning that is intended for description or communication.

Language, to Bruner, is thus central to cognition, fundamental to higher forms of human intelligence and thought. It is language that makes humans human. Such a belief remains very controversial among developmental psychologists; many different and hotly debated theories attempt to define the relationship between thought and language — none is generally predominant, although Bruner's ideas are widely accepted.

The author of a number of textbooks from the later 1940s onward, Bruner reserved perhaps his most significant publication until the 1960s. Particularly characteristic of his theories are *Studies in Cognitive Growth*, written with Rose Olver and Patricia Greenfield and published in 1966, and *Processes of Cognitive Growth*, published in 1968.

ENDOMORPH   ECTOMORPH   MESOMORPH

One of the earliest personality theories attempted to classify individuals into personality types on the basis of body build. A short, plump person (endomorph) was said to be sociable, relaxed, and even-tempered; a tall, thin person (ectomorph) was characterized as restrained, self-conscious, and fond of solitude; and a heavy-set, muscular individual (mesomorph) was described as noisy, callous, and fond of physical activity. Interestingly, those who identify their own "body types" in these categories often also agree with the stereotyped personality ascribed to them.

less attractive — peers. Such self-fulfillment would seem the most likely explanation for the fact that endomorphs, mesomorphs and ectomorphs describe their own personalities in ways which conform to the cultural stereotypes.

There are a number of biological factors which have the potential for influencing personality. Whether they do so, and to what extent, depends upon their interaction with social influences.

Sex Typing

The process by which children come to acquire, value and carry out behavior considered appropriate for one sex but not the other illustrates the nature of some of the social influences on personality and social development in general.

Most of the stereotypic differences between males and females have been found to be invalid. There is evidence, however, that boys are typically more aggressive than girls. And although there is no overall difference in intelligence between the sexes, girls tend to excel in tests of verbal ability whereas boys tend to excel in tests of visuospatial

ability (although there is, of course, enormous overlap between the sexes on these measures).

The origins of such differences, and their consequences, are a major concern of psychologists and of interest to teachers and parents everywhere. There is some evidence of a genetic contribution to differences in visuospatial ability, and several lines of evidence suggest that boys may be biologically predisposed to be more aggressive than girls. This sex difference has been found to hold across cultures and across species. Research with animals has demonstrated that levels of aggression can be increased or reduced by the administration of male and female sex hormones, respectively. For ethical reasons such experiments are obviously not possible with humans.

Most theorists, however, are of the opinion that differential socialization plays a more important role in the development of sex-typed behavior and the individual's sex role identity than genetics, although the latter is not without significance. Consistent with this view is the fact that hermaphrodites (people with both male and female

passive roles, whereas boys are portrayed as the initiators of action.

In these ways, children rapidly come to learn that the consequences of behavior vary as a function of gender. As a result, although both sexes know a great deal about and are capable of carrying out the behavior of either sex, they differ in the frequency with which they carry out these behaviors and the values they attach to them. The danger inherent in these practices is that rigid adherence to sex role stereotypes may prevent individuals from fulfilling their potential.

The Concept of Self

The self is the combination of attributes, values, commitments, social roles and behaviors that are unique to the individual. The growth of the self concept — the cluster of ideas and feelings that a person has about his or her own attributes — involves a slow process of differentiation and elaboration. It thus depends heavily on both cognitive development and all those influences — biological and social — that shape the child's personality. At the same time, the emerging image of self helps to mold the child's future behavior and interactions.

Many developmental theorists believe that newborn infants lack the necessary cognitive maturity to achieve a sense of self. The first step in the development of a sense of separate identity is recognition of the fact that one is separate from objects and other people in the surrounding environment. Observation of infants' behavior suggests that they learn the boundaries of their own bodies during the first four months and recognize that they can act upon objects external to this physical self by about the age of six months. It is not until the age of eighteen to twenty-four months, however, that children show signs of self-recognition when shown their own images in a mirror. For example at this age, but not before, they attempt to remove a spot of rouge applied to their noses.

From age two onward, children increasingly use pronouns such as "I," "me" and "mine" and make a distinction between "I" and "you." This practice suggests that they have a firm concept of self. Initially, this self-concept is anchored in material properties. Pre-schoolers asked to des-

organs) have a sexual identity which is consistent with the sex in which they have been reared, even when this is contrary to their true biological sex.

Parents and others clearly have different criteria by which they reinforce the behavior and responses of boys and girls. These criteria, which reflect cultural sex role stereotypes, relate to clothing and general appearance, body movements, play, career aspirations and vocational choice. Sex-appropriate responses are rewarded; sex-inappropriate ones ignored or even punished.

This differential socialization of boys and girls continues in kindergarten, where some teachers tend to reward girls for passive, dependent behavior and boys for aggressive behavior (by drawing attention to their naughtiness). Boys also tend to receive more help from teachers of a kind that encourages independence and capability than do girls; more often they are shown how to solve problems rather than being provided with the answers.

Cultural sex role stereotypes are also sometimes perpetuated through the media and through children's books in which girls are not only under-represented, but also tend to be portrayed in

Childrens' books provide a rich and powerful source of influence on the young mind. Reading also helps to develop language skills, improving vocabulary and the child's ability to express himself or herself.

Asserting her self-confidence, this child plays teacher to a younger playmate. The playing of such roles is a normal and essential part of mental development and regarded as essential to the recognition of "self."

cribe themselves tend to dwell on their physical characteristics, activities and possessions. As they grow older, commensurate with cognitive development and expanding experience, there is a shift toward a more consciously psychological view of self.

Differences between children in their evaluations of themselves — whether they have high self-esteem (value themselves positively) or low self-esteem (value themselves negatively) — are largely determined by the nature of the feedback they receive from others. Parental attitudes and methods of child-rearing are considered by many experts to be particularly important in this context. They submit that parents who are firm, but accepting, loving and supportive (that is, those who are generally regarded as being authoritative) are more likely to have children who are high in self-esteem, self-reliance and self-control than are parents who are either authoritarian (usually controlling but non-affectionate) or permissive (often warm, but negligent or lax in discipline).

Self-esteem may, in turn, have profound effects on functioning in other areas — especially school achievement and social relationships. These may in turn contribute to the child's overall view of him- or herself. Since there is evidence that low self-esteem is at the root of many psychological problems both during childhood and later in adulthood, the importance of establishing a positive self-concept early in life cannot be overestimated.

During the early years of life, then, human beings progress rapidly from being bundles of reflexes to children with a clear concept of self. It has been shown how nature and nurture interact in every aspect of development, how social experiences are critical to the evolving mind, and how there are both universals of development and individual differences between children from as early as during the first moments of life.

Having recognized the face in the mirror as his own, this young boy, like all young children, experiments with face-pulling. By this means, he can momentarily "change" himself into someone else. With the development of the self concept, children begin to see themselves as individual people, separate from everybody else.

Chapter 3

Thinking and Learning

Experience is an essential factor in the proper development of the mind. A child is not a passive recipient of environmental stimulation, but rather development occurs as the result of his or her interactions with the environment. These themes feature in the following discussion of perception, learning and memory, but there is also a gradual shift in emphasis from the effects of experience that can best be described as "incidental" — that is, resulting from mere exposure — to the effects of more deliberate attempts to "shape" the mind through various forms of learning and education.

Perception — Believing is Perceiving

The study of perception is one of the oldest enterprises in psychology. The earliest psychologists — better called psychophysicists — were concerned largely with such questions as the smallest amount of physical energy necessary for a person to be just able to detect the presence of a stimulus (the "absolute threshold"), and the magnitude of the difference between any two stimuli necessary for a person to be just able to distinguish them from each other (the "just noticeable difference"). There is, however, a great deal more to perception than the physical energy meeting the eyes, ears, skin or any other sense organ, as can be illustrated by the following examples.

People shown the shape of a leaf and of a donkey cut out of identical green cloth and bathed in red light so that both appeared gray, were asked to match the colors of each on a color wheel. They indicated that they perceived the leaf as greener than the donkey.

People presented briefly with "trick" playing cards with colors and suits reversed (as for example a red six of spades) tended either not to perceive the incongruity and thus to report with considerable assurance "the six of hearts," or to offer a compromise response. For example, in the latter case the red six of spades might be reported

The developing mind is sensitive to the effects of a multitude of influencing experiences. The process of learning is probably the most significant shaping factor, because it results in a relatively permanent change in behavior. For this reason, educators continually seek to formulate methods, and devise new materials, to maximize the beneficial effects of learning.

61

as a purple six of hearts or spades, or as a six of spades illuminated by a red light.

Such examples illustrate that perceptual organization is largely determined by expectations built upon past interactions with the environment. How and what we perceive depends not only on the physical stimulation "out there," but also on what we know or believe about a situation. This depends in turn upon contextual cues and past experiences. Some experiences are common to members of the same culture — hence our propensity for seeing things as others around us do most of the time. Other experiences are more or less unique to ourselves.

Wine tasters, for example, are able to distinguish differences between wines which most other people are unable to detect because they lack the appropriate learning experiences. Similarly, most blind people are better than sighted people at utilizing auditory cues: they can make more accurate judgments of distance on the basis of sounds echoing back from distant surfaces. The same ability prevents them from walking into obstacles such as walls — an ability which is disrupted if

their ears are plugged. Interestingly, blind people are often unaware that they are using auditory cues for this purpose, believing rather that they are responding to tactile stimulation.

That perception is an active process, not simply a mirror of some external reality, can be illustrated by situations in which the pattern of stimulation reaching the senses is ambiguous. Consider, for example, the well-known Necker cube. As we stare at the cube, the nearest face suddenly turns out to be possibly the farthest. Another, more dramatic example of this phenomenon is Boring's wife/mother-in-law picture. As we stare at this drawing, the image of a young woman alternates with that of an old hag. Such instances illustrate the point made by the British scientist Richard Gregory that "Perception is a matter of selecting appropriate hypotheses of external objects according to prevailing information."

Most of the time, the prevailing information or contextual cues available enable us rapidly to reach a decision concerning the nature of the stimulus. In cases like the Necker cube, however, the situation is ambiguous, so we perceive reversals as the

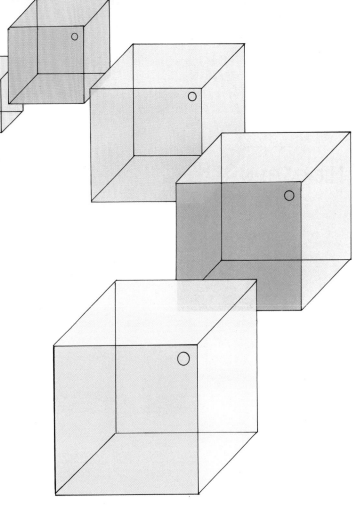

In this famous illusion devised by L. A. Necker, the tinted surfaces of the cubes appear to alternate in depth. The mind's visual system entertains alternative hypotheses but never settles on one solution.

brain alternately tests different hypotheses. The ability of the human mind to store and make use of past experience in interpreting the physical stimulation reaching the senses for the most part ensures greater efficiency in our perception. Occasionally, however, it can "lead us astray," as in the case of some of the perceptual illusions.

Perceptual Constancy

We perceive a circular plate as round regardless of the angle from which we view it, and despite the fact that as we change position the image of the plate on the retina of the eye changes shape, becoming more or less elliptical. Similarly, we continue to perceive a man as the same height whether he is ten or twenty feet away from us, despite a reduction in the size of the retinal image as he moves farther away. Snow continues to look white and coal to look black despite changes in illumination; and we tend to continue to perceive our own, familiar, cars as the same color whether we view them in daylight or under yellow street lamps at nighttime.

This stability of perception in the face of variation in physical stimulation is termed perceptual constancy. It depends on our ability to take into account the circumstances of stimulation and to compensate accordingly. This has obvious significance for biological survival. Without the mechanisms of constancy, our sensory experiences would be continually changing and our world would be utterly chaotic.

The compensatory processes operating to permit such constancy in perceived size can be readily observed if you produce an afterimage by staring for a few seconds at a bright light or a black spot on a white page, then look first at a near surface, then at surfaces farther away. As you view the more distant surfaces the afterimage appears to increase in size. The brain is compensating for the reduction in the size of the retinal image which usually occurs when an object is viewed from an increasing distance.

Although infants demonstrate size and shape constancy to some extent, the constancies continue to develop with age and experience. People who have been blind from birth and who have had their sight restored as adults show little evidence of

constancy initially. Further evidence that the constancies develop through experience is the finding of a breakdown in size constancy among people living in heavily forested country in the African Congo, where distances scanned rarely exceed 450 yards. Placed for the first time in open country, these people perceived buffaloes grazing some distance away as "insects," and a boat some distance from the shore as a scrap of wood floating on the water.

The constancies illustrate dramatically that perception depends not just on the pattern of stimulation reaching the eye, but also on our interpretation of the entire situation. This is almost entirely dependent on past experience.

Confusing the Brain

Constancies refer to the fact that we tend to see things as they really are, even when the stimulation reaching the senses is changing. Illusions, in contrast, are distortions of reality. Like the constancies, however, illusions reflect the fact that perception does not passively mirror sensory input, but is an active process influenced by past

The two lines comprising the Müller-Lyer illusion (below) are the same length although most people see the left-hand line as longer because of the tendency to interpret the figures as three-dimensional objects.

Individuals who grow up in the right-angled layout of Western society should, in theory, be more susceptible to the illusion than those living in a non-rectangular environment (bottom).

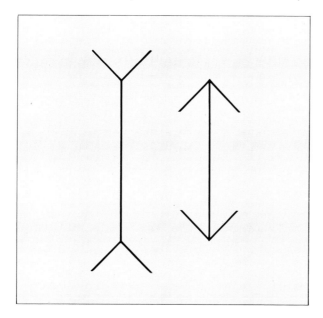

experience. Some illusions may depend on the same underlying mechanisms as the constancies: they may be examples of "misplaced constancy."

An illusion which clearly illustrates the role of learning and past experience in perception is the trapezoidal window devised by Adelbert Ames. The trapezoidal window is painted on both sides to give the impression of a rectangular window turned at an angle. It is mounted on a rod connected to a motor which rotates it at a slow constant speed. Observed from a distance of about twenty feet, it is perceived not as a rotating trapezoid, but as an oscillating rectangular window. This can be attributed to the fact that in the course of our experience, the image cast upon the retina by a rectangular window is more often than not trapezoidal (it is rectangular only when we are facing the window head on). We have learned to interpret these trapezoidal images as rectangular.

Given that the trapezoidal window is perceived as rectangular, it follows that the character of the movement must be seen as oscillation because the continuous array of images produced on the retina could occur only from a rectangular surface that oscillates; the perception of rotation would be inconsistent with the assumption that the window is rectangular. Zulus, whose culture is not only devoid of windows, but also of surfaces with right-angles, straight lines and other cues of rectangularity, experience the illusion to a lesser extent than most other people.

Among illusions that have been attributed to misplaced constancy is the "Ponzo" or railroad tracks illusion. If two parallel lines of equal length are drawn horizontally across a pair of converging lines drawn vertically, the uppermost of the parallel lines appears longer. The greater the cues to depth, the greater the illusion, as in the case of parallel horizontal lines drawn across converging railroad tracks. This illusion can be attributed to the brain's attempt to compensate for the expected shrinkage of images with increasing apparent distance. Because in this instance there is no shrinkage, the uppermost of the horizontal lines appears to be slightly longer.

That past experience determines the extent of this illusion is indicated by the fact that it increases from childhood to adulthood, and by evidence that

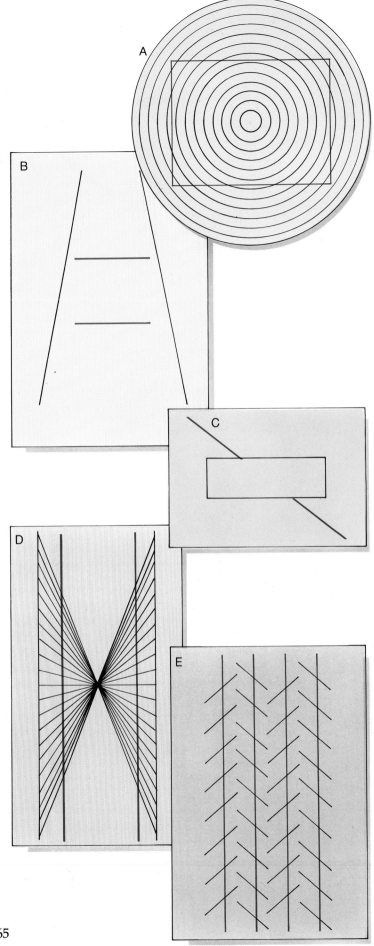

Visual illusions mislead the mind. The central figure in A is a true rectangle and the horizontal lines in B have equal length. The line in C is straight, and the vertical lines in D and E are parallel.

rural populations in Uganda show the illusion to a lesser extent than urban populations who have had more exposure to pictorial depth. This finding suggests not only that the experience of pictorial depth is a prerequisite for perceiving illusions of depth, but also that perception of depth in flat pictures requires some kind of learning process.

Another well-known illusion which may rely for its effect on misplaced constancy is the Müller-Lyer illusion, in which the apparent length of two equal lines is distorted by the addition of arrow heads pointing inward and outward. It has been suggested that the arrow heads provide false distance cues.

Illusions can occur in any of the senses; they also occur across the senses. An example of the latter is the so-called "size-weight illusion," which refers to the fact that small objects feel considerably heavier than larger objects of the same weight. This compelling illusion is easily demonstrated by placing the same weight of sand in a small can and in a larger can. Observers will report that the small can weighs up to fifty per cent more. What this illusion demonstrates is that the weight of an object is perceived not only according to pressure on muscle senses, but also according to its expected weight based on visually judged size. Past experience tells us that objects which look larger usually tend to weigh more than smaller ones. When, on the basis of visual appearance, density is unexpected, the illusion of additional weight is experienced.

The Effects of Needs and Motives

We tend to see and hear what we want to see and hear as well as what we expect to see and hear. Our needs and motives affect the choice of objects perceived (that is, which aspects of our environment we selectively attend to) and the clarity and accuracy with which they are perceived (in the direction of either improved accuracy or greater distortion).

Some experiments relating to these notions have suggested differences in the primary motives of men and women. For example, there is a tendency for the pupils of males to dilate in response to pictures of nude females, whereas the pupils of females dilate in response to pictures of babies.

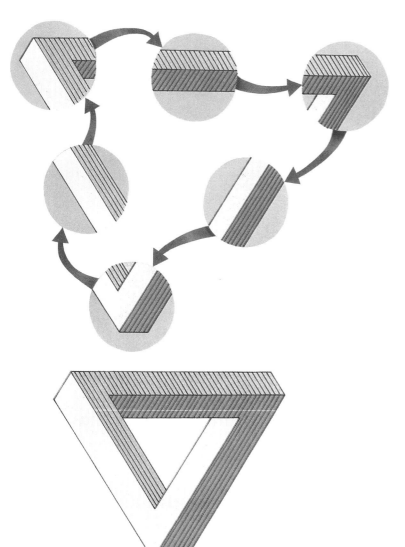

motivational factors and the meaning of the situation for the person concerned. For example, during religious ceremonies — but not at other times — dervishes can endure extremely painful stimulation, such as that produced by walking on burning coals, with apparent tranquility. Similarly, the celebrant of the hook-swinging ceremony practiced in some parts of India is able to hang suspended from steel hooks embedded in his back, as he blesses children and crops, without showing any evidence of pain. Mothers seldom report feeling the injection given shortly after the birth of a baby to facilitate detachment of the afterbirth. Men injured in battle apparently experience less pain than people with comparable tissue damage resulting from surgery during peacetime.

A need which appears to be common to us all is the need for an optimal level of stimulation. Given choice, we attend to aspects of our environment which are moderately complex and novel, and it is under these circumstances that our perceptual systems appear to function best. The effects of too little or too much stimulation are dramatic and unequivocal. Anecdotal evidence, such as that from prisoners in solitary confinement, Arctic explorers and radar operators, and findings from experimental studies of the effects of sensory deprivation have indicated that being deprived of adequate stimulation results in intellectual disruption, severe emotional disturbances and perceptual distortions such as hallucinations. Students were unable to tolerate conditions of sensory deprivation for longer than a maximum of three days, despite considerable financial inducements to do so. Too much, or excessively complex stimulation can also disrupt behavior. Exactly what constitutes too little or too much, too simple or too complex stimulation varies between individuals and depends on both a person's constitutional makeup and his or her past history.

Shaping the Mind Through Learning

A first step in understanding how controlled experience affects behavior is the study of learning. Learning occurs when there is a change in behavior resulting from experience. Behavior changes caused by fatigue, arousal or maturation are not learning. If a complaining acquaintance

Hungry people are more sensitive to food-related items than to non-food-related items. As time since the last meal increases, within certain limits, pictures of food need to be less bright in order to be discriminated than do pictures of, say, household articles. On the whole, pleasant events tend to be more readily perceived than are unpleasant events.

Similarly, the ease and manner with which we perceive various stimuli depend upon their relationship to our personal needs and values. This has been clearly demonstrated in the case of racially prejudiced subjects who, when shown a picture of a black face to one eye and a white face to the other through a binocular stereoscope, tend to perceive either a black face or a white face. This is in contrast to the experience of non-prejudiced people, who tend to fuse the two faces and report seeing a combined face.

The perception of pain is also influenced by

The ingenious use of reversible
figures and ground makes the
painting Heaven and Hell by M. C.
Escher a truly remarkable work of art.
The dozens of angels and devils,
gradually diminishing in size, can be
seen to alternate, but neither seems to
dominate the other.

makes fewer nagging comments than he or she did previously, it is the result of learning only if he or she has the experience that nagging does not achieve a goal. Learning has not occurred if the nagger has simply become tired of making comments or has fallen asleep.

Unfortunately, learning cannot be measured directly; instead, scientists usually count how often a particular response is performed (for example, nagging). There is an assumed correlation between learning and performance — that is, the incidence count.

If a stimulus event is repeated often enough so that we no longer seem to notice it, habituation is said to occur. This can be checked by changing the stimulus so that renewed notice is taken (dishabituation), or omitting it, which rearouses attention to the stimulus. An example is waking when an express train passes nearby at 2 a.m. each night. After a few nights' experience, we no longer wake up when it goes by, unless a slow freight train replaces it, and then we notice that the usual event is no longer happening. We also notice if the train is canceled and may wake when it does not make its usual noise. This sort of behavior change is related to perceptual processing because we build up a scheme of expected, regular stimulation. It is only when the expectation is not met that we become aware that we are still attempting to process the stimulus.

Classical conditioning is another way in which we respond to stimuli that occur regularly. The Russian psychologist Ivan Pavlov (1849–1936) first isolated this sort of learning by noting that dogs eventually began to salivate to a buzzer which regularly preceded a presentation of food, rather than waiting until the food was present. The occurrence of the response, salivation, is said to be "conditioned" to the buzzer. Conditioning takes place only if the buzzer (a conditioned stimulus)

Ivan Pavlov

Reflections on Reflex

Ivan Petrovich Pavlov is well known as the discoverer of the "conditioned reflex" through his experiments with dogs. Less well known is that he was first famous for research into the circulation of the blood, and received the Nobel prize for describing his work on the physiology of digestion.

Pavlov was born in Ryazan, about 100 miles south-east of Moscow, in September 1849. The son of a priest, his first intention was also to enter the ministry, but after four years at a theological college he decided he had no vocation and instead in 1870 went to the University of St Petersburg (now Leningrad) to study chemistry and physiology. It was not until 1879, however, that he received his medical degree; his doctorate came four years later, from the Military Academy. The next two years were spent studying abroad (in present-day East Germany and Poland) under eminent physiologists. Then, returning to St Petersburg, he carried out research for a time before he was appointed Professor of Pharmacology at the Imperial Medical Academy in 1890, and a year later Director of the Physiology Department for Experimental Medicine. Much of the work for which he is now renowned was carried out in the subsequent decade.

Despite being an outspoken anti-Communist, Pavlov stayed in the Soviet Union after the Revolution, not only tolerated by the government — which lionized him — but pressed by it into accepting funds and premises for his work. In 1922 he requested permission to emigrate; it was refused. Two years later he resigned his professorship — but continued his research until at least the age of eighty-five.

Pavlov's initial research into digestion elucidated the function of the nerves in the pancreas that cause the secretion of pancreatic enzymes. By introducing false gastric vessels into a dog's alimentary system he was able to measure the amount of digestive secretions produced by the sight or smell of food, to discern the importance of the vagus nerve to gastric secretions, and to discover that the secretions are constant in acidity.

This work in turn led him on to testing the responses of dogs conditioned to expect food — and so salivate — following the ringing of a bell. Such a conditioned reflex was experimentally determined to depend on the integrity of the cerebral cortex.

Pavlov went on to suggest — rightly or wrongly, it is still a matter for debate — that much of learning, particularly in humans the habituation of moral behavior, is derived as conditioned reflexes adopted from earliest childhood onward.

This theory forms the basis of modern Soviet physiological studies; it remains controversial in the West, where the structure and functioning of the nervous system has probably come under closer scientific scrutiny. But it has had considerable influence in psychology and psychiatry, and in the field of education, despite being contrary to Freudian precepts.

Pavlov was awarded many international honors, and his writings appeared in several languages. He died in Leningrad in February 1936.

and food (an unconditioned stimulus) occur near to each other in time, and only if the buzzer reliably predicts the food. When the pairing of the buzzer and food breaks down, then extinction is said to occur and the conditioned response (salivation) is no longer elicited.

Classical conditioning can be shown in many animals, as well as in humans, and for many responses. For instance, the sight of a German shepherd dog may elicit sweating and other stress responses in a mailman who has been bitten by such a dog. Experiences such as this may even be the basis of phobic reactions.

When seeing a German shepherd is no longer predictive of (or in close temporal proximity to) being bitten — that is, when the mailman has encountered many such dogs which have not bitten him — the mailman will no longer sweat when he finds himself in this situation.

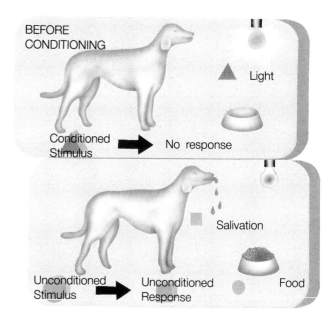

Operant Conditioning

A voluntary response made more frequently after a rewarding experience has followed it is a result of operant conditioning. Likewise, such responses decrease when the reward is withheld; the process of extinction. This sort of learning has doubtless occurred since the advent of mankind. When a knight chanced to look at a fair damsel, and she rewarded him with a twinkle in her eye, he was more likely to look at her again. Almost any behavior can be conditioned in this way, even some verbal and creative responses. However, the landmark research on operant conditioning was carried out by the American experimental psychologist B. F. Skinner. Operant conditioning has been clearly demonstrated in many vertebrates, but white rats, pigeons, and young adult humans are the favorite subjects for laboratory investigations.

If a desired response to a stimulus does not occur spontaneously, then a shaping procedure can be used; that is, responses which successively approximate the finally desired one are rewarded. Thus a hungry rat can first be trained to go over near a lever, then to touch it, and eventually to press it because each step is rewarded in turn (with food). Through shaping by successive approximation, a young child can be toilet-trained. A long behavioral chain of responses is conditioned using operant methods, including distinguishing a sense of urgency, going to an appropriate place, removing clothes, and correctly using a potty.

There are various types of operant conditioning techniques. A response can be strengthened by following it with a positive reinforcement (a reward), or by removing a negative reinforcement (an aversive event). For example, a pupil can learn to spell a difficult word if doing so results in receiving a good grade or averting punishment.

If there are stimulus conditions which predict when an aversive event will occur, and the animal responds during this stimulus, it is called avoidance. For example, if a rat perceives the smell of a predator (stimulus), it can hide in a hole which is too small for the predator to enter (avoidance response). If there are no stimuli present which predict an aversive event, then there is an escape situation.

In some cases in which a discriminative stimulus is available to signal reinforcement, this stimulus itself may take on rewarding properties. This is called a secondary reinforcer. For example, for humans money is a "conditioned" or secondary reinforcer for other primary rewards such as food. People will work for money itself, even if there is little that can be bought with it. Robinson Crusoe even hid the gold from his shipwrecked vessel

70

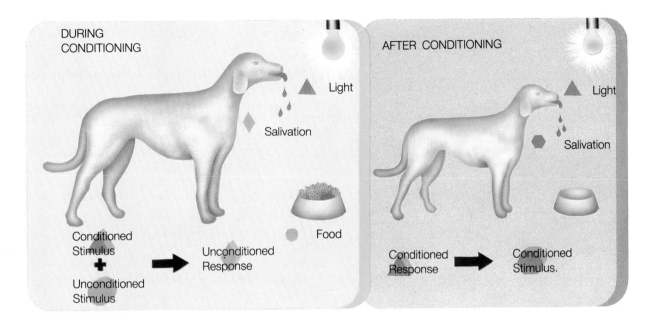

DURING CONDITIONING

Light

Salivation

Food

Conditioned
Stimulus
+
Unconditioned
Stimulus

Unconditioned
Response

AFTER CONDITIONING

Light

Salivation

Conditioned
Response

Conditioned
Stimulus.

despite believing that he was on an uninhabited island. The author Daniel Defoe knew that his readers would understand how the hero had been conditioned to see value in the gold itself. Most learning situations have an element of secondary reinforcement.

All such procedures for operant conditioning are affected by the schedule for reinforcement. If the reinforcement occurs on only some trials, then the response not only becomes more frequent. In addition, the response also becomes more resistant to extinction. Thus buying ice cream for a child (a reinforcement) only on some of the occasions when it is requested (the response) increases the frequency of requests for this treat. If the partial reinforcement comes in a temporal pattern, for example, when a reward is available after each five minutes has passed (a fixed-interval schedule of reinforcement), then the response pattern mimics the reward pattern. Thus on fixed-interval schedules there is a pause in responding following each reinforcement, giving way to gradual increase in responding up to the next reward.

Looking for a bus scheduled for every half hour is an example. A person does not look for it right after one has passed, but there is a great deal of bus searching as the half-hour fixed interval is nearly over. Variable-interval schedules of rein-

Learning is fundamental to understanding behavior. Making a new association or connection between events in the environment is the most basic form of learning of which classical conditioning, first demonstrated by the physiologist Ivan Pavlov, represents one such type. Pavlov noticed that a dog began to salivate at the mere sight of a food dish. The dog had learned to associate the sight of the dish with the taste and the smell of food. Subsequent pairings of a light with food during conditioning caused the dog to salivate (as a conditioned response) on presentation of the light alone.

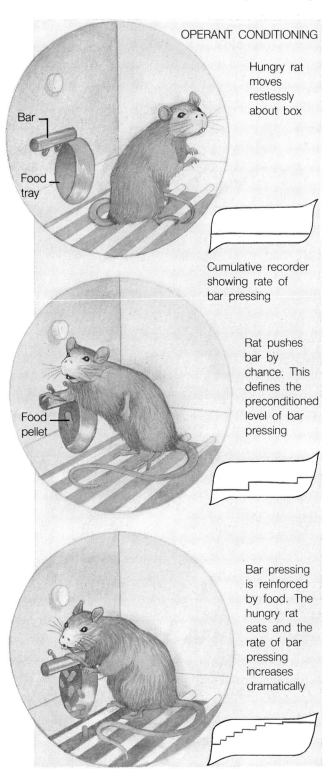

The operant conditioning approach to learning developed from B. F. Skinner's pioneering studies with rats in the 1930s. Using a specially designed cage, known as a Skinner box, he observed the rate at which a hungry rat pressed a bar to obtain food. From this came the basic premise: an organism learns that a particular response (bar pressing) leads to a particular consequence (food as a reinforcement of that act).

OPERANT CONDITIONING

Bar

Food tray

Hungry rat moves restlessly about box

Cumulative recorder showing rate of bar pressing

Food pellet

Rat pushes bar by chance. This defines the preconditioned level of bar pressing

Bar pressing is reinforced by food. The hungry rat eats and the rate of bar pressing increases dramatically

forcement give rise to more regular responding. Thus, looking for cabs which appear at variable times occurs at a constant rate (without pauses).

There are some similarities between classical and operant conditioning. One similar feature is generalization. If a dog salivates because a high-pitched tone signifies the approach of food, then tones near the critical one in pitch will elicit salivation, but the rate of salivation decreases with the increase in pitch difference from the original. Similar findings occur in operant conditioning.

A procedure which weakens a response is punishment. An aversive event that occurs after a given response results in a reduction in the behavior, so long as the punishing event is strong. For instance, an investor will probably stop buying stock if he loses a lot of money on some recent investments. Milder punishments may reduce the behavior for a while, but subsequently it may increase. For example, children may stop taking cookies if the response is a mild reprimand. However, a recoil effect is often seen: a day later more cookies than before may be taken.

One reaction to punishment that has been studied is called a conditioned emotional response. A stimulus present when a strong aversive event occurs elicits many of the stress behaviors connected with the punishment, such as running away or remaining immobile, "frozen with fear." For example, if a man is exposed to a siren before a bomb goes off, he will almost certainly show some stress symptoms when he next hears that siren.

Applications of Conditioning

There are many applications of conditioning principles for both animals and humans. Training guide dogs for blind or deaf people is an example of ways that behavior chains and stimulus control can be made useful. The dogs (and owners) have learned complex sequences of behavior, using operant and classical conditioning techniques.

Some human applications of conditioning can be seen in factories and in the community. For instance, a worker in a chocolate factory might be watching candies as they pass along a conveyor belt. Whenever a defective candy is spotted, this causes dishabituation. The worker is conditioned to remove the bad candy from the belt.

In a community context, the collection of trash is an example of the application of conditioning. In states where a small monetary deposit is returned if empty cans are placed in an appropriate receptacle, there is much less can litter. It is interesting that the small reward, often only five cents per can, is a more effective reinforcer than social conscience — a preference for a tidy landscape — or the imposition of a fine for leaving litter.

Constraints of Conditioning

Although conditioning theory embraces a broad range of behavior, other theories of cognition and motivation are also required to explain an organism's ability to learn. Insight learning, or the capacity to form mental sets for achieving a goal, as described by the German psychologist Wolfgang Köhler, is an important example. Monkeys which solve problems by using objects as tools provide an example of this type of learning. For instance, in

Animals such as this lion can be taught complex tricks by means of shaping techniques. These involve reinforcing, usually by means of a reward, only those responses that meet the trainer's specifications, and extinguishing others by withholding the reward.

"A watched pot never boils" is an old adage that may have some foundation in learning theory. By going away and doing something else, it is likely that on your return the pot will be boiling.

one experiment a monkey could obtain bananas suspended from the ceiling by piling up some boxes in the room to function as a stepping stool. The monkey successfully reached the bananas, but it had not received reinforcement for each successive approximation of the box-piling behavior, so this insight learning does not seem to be accounted for by principles of operant conditioning.

Other constraints on explaining events in terms of conditioning involve species-specific responses, such as the response of not eating a poisonous substance or, by humans, of learning language. Animals who are given poisoned food show disgust when offered that food again, even if there are several hours between eating the food and being ill. Such a long delay is outside the time limits for effective classical conditioning.

Human language learning is also not fully encompassed by conditioning theory. Rather, it is

hypothesized that a "deep structure" underlies the syntactic and grammatical rules that govern language. Even before the use of these rules is explicitly reinforced, they are apparent in the speech of three-year-old children.

Mechanisms of Memory

The central role of memory in the processes of learning — and indeed perception — is especially evident in the case of people who have some memory deficit. It is common for concussion or head-injury patients to lose their memory for events immediately preceding the injury, although their memory for events in the more distant past remains intact. This condition, called retrograde amnesia, is one piece of evidence suggesting that it may be justifiable to distinguish between two types of memory. Short-term memory applies to situations in which material needs to be remembered for only a matter of seconds (as, for example,

The recall of lists is greatly improved when all items are in some way connected in memory. This is the main principle behind many mnemonic (memory-aiding) systems. One famous mnemonic system is called the method of loci, in which items from a list are imagined in various locations throughout a mental walk in a familiar environment. They can be recalled by taking the mental walk again.

METHOD OF LOCI

when we need to remember a telephone number just long enough to be able to dial it). Long-term memory involves material that has been retained for any time from a matter of minutes to a number of decades.

Both short- and long-term memory involve three stages — encoding, storage, and retrieval — but the nature of these processes differs in each case.

Spoken material is encoded in short-term memory (STM) primarily according to its acoustic properties. Scientists know this from studies of the sorts of errors people make when asked to recall strings of letters with which they have just been presented. When they make mistakes, the incorrect letters tend to sound similar to the correct one (they might recall C instead of T).

A visual code may also be used by STM, particularly when the to-be-remembered stimuli are pictures which are difficult to describe. Some individuals have a so-called "photographic mem-

ory" (more correctly termed eidetic imagery). Such people can hold in short-term memory visual images that are so clear as to be like photographs. Eidetic imagery is rare, and for most of us the acoustic code is dominant in short-term memory.

The dominant code in long-term memory (LTM) appears to be semantic — that is, it is based on the meaning of items. Again, this is known from the sorts of errors people make when recalling items from LTM. Erroneously recalled words, for example, tend to be similar in meaning to the correct items (for example, "quick" instead of "fast"). An imagery code may also be used in LTM.

In contrast to LTM, which has an almost infinite capacity, the storage capacity of STM is limited to about seven items. This capacity can be greatly increased by organizing material into meaningful units or "chunks," such as letters into words, or words into sentences. The capacity remains about seven chunks. Material can be retained in STM and ultimately transferred to LTM, thus preventing the encoding of new material. The major cause of forgetting in STM is displacement of old by new items, which occurs if the old items are not repeatedly rehearsed.

Given that its limits are not exceeded, retrieval from STM is usually fairly effortless and error free. This again contrasts with retrieval from LTM, which tends to be error prone. Difficulties in retrieval are a major cause of "forgetting" in LTM. People who have experienced the "tip-of-the-tongue" phenomenon, or who have been unable to recall the answer to an examination question only to have it pop into their heads as soon as they leave the examination hall, are only too well aware

"Run Off You Girls, Boys In View"
is a useful mnemonic device for
recalling the colors of the rainbow. It
works by constructing a meaningful
sentence out of words that start with
the initial letters of the colors.

of the fact that material can be stored in memory and yet be inaccessible.

Under special circumstances, emotion may interfere with memory. Extremely disturbing memories may be almost impossible to retrieve without the help of therapeutic intervention. These usually relate to traumatic events which, because of their painful associations have been "repressed" and actively blocked from consciousness. However, even though they remain unconscious, they may give rise to psychological problems such as "free-floating" anxiety (anxiety not related to any particular object) or depression. For mental health to be restored, these memories may have to be brought into consciousness, so that the emotions associated with them can be "worked through" to resolution.

Another cause of difficulty in retrieval from LTM is interference—of new material with old (retroactive inhibition) and vice versa (proactive inhibi-

tion). The more similar the two sets of material, the greater is the interference. This is one reason why material learned shortly before going to sleep is better retained than that followed by the learning of other material; there is less chance of interference. Students studying for examinations might be well advised to intersperse the learning of relevant material with totally different activities to minimize the chances of interference.

What we recall is also affected by mood. Recent research has shown that depressed individuals tend to recall many more unhappy memories than happy ones; the discrepancy reduces as their mood improves. On the other hand, people in whom a happy mood has been induced more readily recall pleasant events than events which have been unpleasant ones.

Memory, as demonstrated by the British psychologist Frederic Bartlett, is constructive. This can be illustrated by the well-known party game

which involves one person whispering a short story to another who, in turn, recounts it to a third person and so on. By the time the story has reached the tenth person it may be quite unrecognizable from the original. Particularly if we cannot hear perfectly, we tend to drop details that make no sense to us, and to add details that make the story more meaningful.

Recollections of events are also influenced by the inferences we make, and by the stereotypes we hold. This has important implications for eye-witness accounts of events such as traffic accidents. For example, in one study people were shown a film of a traffic accident and later asked questions about it. People who were asked how fast the cars were going when they "smashed" into each other were more likely to recall having seen broken glass (even though there was none) than were people asked how fast the cars were going when they merely "hit" each other. This illustrates how research findings relating to memory may have practical value.

It is possible to improve memory? Organization of material is one way of improving retrieval from long-term memory as well as from STM. For example, it is usually easier to remember many more of a list of words if we recall them by category rather than randomly. The more the material we store is organized, the easier it is to retrieve. Being in the same context, or recalling the context in which learning took place, also facilitates retrieval. So too does practicing retrieval while learning material.

Long-term memory can also be improved at the encoding stage, for example by expanding on the meaning of to-be-remembered material and by using imagery. This latter method — one of a number of so-called "mnemonic devices" — has been found to be particularly effective for facilitating the learning of foreign languages.

As yet science knows little about the kinds of changes in the brain that mediate the encoding and storage of memories. Various physiological and biochemical changes have been proposed, but research in the field is still in its infancy.

The Meaning of Intelligence

The ability to learn and remember depends on intelligence. To some of us an intelligent person is

Intelligence tests were first formulated by the French psychologist Alfred Binet. A sample from his original test (bottom) required children to complete a series of unfinished pictures.

one who is bright, someone capable of learning about academic subjects easily. To others, intelligence is synonymous with the score in an intelligence test. Both of these ideas are oversimplifications. For instance, in any given individual there are variations among different tasks. A bricklayer may be adept at solving a practical three-dimensional problem, whereas an editor may be more able to choose written material that will sell well in several months' time. Neither person is necessarily quick to solve the other's problem.

Modern psychologists define intelligence as the general capacity to learn, reason and solve problems. The ability to profit from experience and think in an abstract way must be therefore complemented by a similar ability to motivate oneself and to adapt to changes.

Intelligence Tests

Extensive investigations have been made into the subject of intelligence tests. For example, does the score on an intelligence test remain stable over a person's life? Do test scores predict future job and school success? How do genetic and environmental events interact in measures of intelligence?

Intelligence tests are composed of questions which attempt to measure the way people solve certain problems, often divided into questions relating to mathematical, verbal and spatial abilities. A high score on such a test should reflect a good approach to problem solving, not prior knowledge of the material. Language skills, education and test-taking techniques can, however, contribute to better scores. This is known as socio-cultural bias, because people from cultures that do not emphasize these skills find it more difficult to attain high scores.

The final score achieved in an intelligence test is called an intelligence quotient, or IQ, and is determined by comparing an individual's ability to that of a large reference group of people in his or her age range on whom the test was standardized. Within any given age range, an IQ between 90 and 109 is considered average. A study of ''geniuses,'' people with IQs of 135 plus, showed they had attained higher levels of educational achievement, higher incomes, and greater success at their chosen occupation than the average for that occu-

Every note played by this robot is executed by a string of commands that have been programmed into its complex electronic "brain." Whereas the endurance and mass computational power of such machines may be superior to that of humans, research has still not enabled the development of a machine that is capable of thinking.

pation. Thus, in these ways, IQ test scores may be said to predict success in later life.

Generally, IQ scores are more valuable as predictors for younger test-takers. Tests given in kindergarten predict success in later schooling about 45 per cent of the time; tests given in grade school, about 30 per cent of the time; tests given in college account for only about 16 per cent of the variation of success at graduate school. An exception to this rule is that tests given to children up to six or seven years old are not very predictive of later IQs nor of later school success (accounting for only 4 per cent of academic success at kindergarten). This may be because infant tests tend to examine the motor and cognitive skills of development in contrast to the usual written materials used for school-age intelligence tests.

Both genetic and environmental factors play a part in the outcome of intelligence tests. Concordance in IQ between family members argues in favor of genetic influence. The stronger the genetic link, the greater is the correlation between IQ scores. Identical twins have very similar scores about 80 per cent of the time; fraternal twins, about 55 per cent of the time; and brothers and sisters about 25 per cent of the time. The rate of concordance between parent and child IQs is similar to that for brothers and sisters.

The importance of environment is demonstrated by two types of research: studies of twins and studies of enrichment programs for "disadvantaged" children. In twin studies, there is a greater correlation between identical twin pairs who are reared together (correlation of about 0.90) than between pairs reared separately (about 0.75). Similarly, the correlation between brothers and sisters on IQ is greater if they are reared together (0.49) than apart (0.46).

Schemes for preschoolers, such as Head Start, which use organized play, early reading exercises and other techniques for intellectual stimulation have been shown to produce improvement of ten to fifteen points on the IQ scores of "disadvantaged" children. Subsequently, the children with improved scores displayed less antisocial behavior in school and better success in the job market than their contemporaries who did not receive the extra early stimulation. However, the effectiveness of

James McKeen Cattell

Bringing Objectivity to the Subject

A leading psychologist in his time and an extremely competent journalist and author, James Cattell seems to have been possessed of one overwhelming trait: he loved to fully investigate whatever took his interest. This led him not only to devise a series of tests to measure the mental abilities of students, but also to apply the knowledge gained to the field of education and then to advertising and other commercial enterprises.

Cattell was born in May 1860 in Easton, Pennsylvania; he grew up and was educated there, graduating from Lafayette College at the age of twenty. He then spent more than a year in Germany studying philosophy and psychology at the Universities of Göttingen and Leipzig, before returning to study psychology further at Johns Hopkins University, Baltimore. This occupied 1882 and 1883, for part of which time he was under the direction of the eminent psychologist G. Stanley Hall. In the following year he went back to Leipzig University, becoming assistant to his former teacher Wilhelm Wundt, celebrated for experimental psychology. It was there in 1886 that Cattell received his doctorate. Nevertheless, one year later he was working in London,

England, in Francis Galton's laboratory, and Galton's strong ideas on anthropology and the genetic transmission of intelligence also intrigued Cattell greatly.

So well traveled and of such wide acquaintance with eminent scientists, it is perhaps no wonder that in 1888 Cattell was invited to become the first Professor of Psychology at the University of Pennsylvania in Philadelphia. But after only three years in the post he left to become Professor (and administrative head) of Psychology at Columbia University, New York, where he stayed for twenty-six years. Then, in 1917, he publicly criticized the enlistment of conscripts to go to fight in World War I — and was

dismissed. By this time, however, he had already founded a number of periodical scientific journals, to which he was now able to devote all his energies. These included *Scientific Monthly*, which he edited until 1943, and *The American Naturalist*, of which he was editor right up to his death, in January 1944.

Cattell used his talent for investigation most profitably as Wundt's assistant in Leipzig. He first of all redesigned much of the apparatus in the laboratory to improve its function. Inventing his own equipment, he then also carried out original research into aspects of psychology which are closely related to physiology — such as the measurement of the interval between stimulus and reaction, and the effect on it of varying intensity of the stimulus. Scientific objectivity in this field was rare in those days, and Cattell's research was almost unique in separating psychology from the discipline of philosophy. A year after his time with Galton, Cattell established a laboratory at Philadelphia in which his tests for measuring students' mental abilities were devised and carried out. For a time such testing became the focus of his career, although it was not until 1921 that he founded the Psychological Corporation.

Drawing gives children the opportunity to express themselves through color and form. This encourages the use of imagery, which is thought to contribute to the development of creative thinking.

If a creativity test asks: "What uses can you think of for a can?", one answer might be to make it into a simple oil lamp. It is creative if the product is also useful and aesthetically pleasing.

Head Start depended partly on whether the parents of these children became involved, and there is considerable controversy over how important genetic and environmental factors are in the ten-to-fifteen-point discrepancy.

Another debate concerns the use of IQ tests. If IQ scores help to make the teaching environment more appropriate for each pupil's needs, then they have a valuable function. The first intelligence tests invented by the Frenchman Alfred Binet were designed to choose which pupils would most benefit from education. On the other hand, the use of intelligence test scores to stereotype and track children because of their social or racial characteristics, and which fails to take account of individual and task differences, is destructive.

Alternative Approaches

One alternative to quantifying intelligence by test scores is the characterization of intelligence according to the stages of cognitive development proposed by Jean Piaget. He described the progress of a child from concrete to abstract stages of thinking. Educational tasks can, in turn, be tailored to the individual's stage of development.

Other approaches separate intelligence into clusters of related individual skills. Thus, some researchers stress the difference between theoretical and practical capabilities, or between crystallized (accumulated knowledge) and fluid (problem-solving) intelligence.

Many modern psychologists separate the ability to reason into components, each concerned with one aspect of information processing. For instance, mathematical, musical and linguistic skills can be regarded as quite independent abilities. And it is possible to divide these individual skills even further. For example, one linguistic skill such as reading can be separated into many components which include the ability to blend sounds, convert visual symbols into auditory representations, and the ability to remember visual images.

The variety of approaches to the study of intelligence shows that the mind comprises many interacting facets. There may be some general ability to reason and learn, but variations within this ability are enormous. There are some elements of intelligence which suggest a hereditary influence and

some that indicate environmental effects. Research has made it abundantly clear that intelligence is far from being a simple concept.

Conceptualizing Creativity

Creativity is an aspect of intelligence that is not measured by standard intelligence tests. It is difficult to define, but most definitions focus on originality, emphasizing at the same time the requirement of usefulness or aesthetic satisfaction. It is clear from research findings that although a lack of general intelligence, as assessed by IQ tests, would impose severe restraints upon creative achievements, high intelligence is no guarantee of creativity. Beyond an IQ of about 120, there is little relationship between intelligence and creativity.

What are the characteristics that distinguish creative from noncreative individuals? In seeking to answer this question, research has tended to concentrate on personality attributes on the one hand, and on the cognitive abilities, thinking styles and intellectual processes involved in creativity on the other.

The notion of a "creative personality" has captured the imagination of lay people and psychologists alike, not least because of the popular

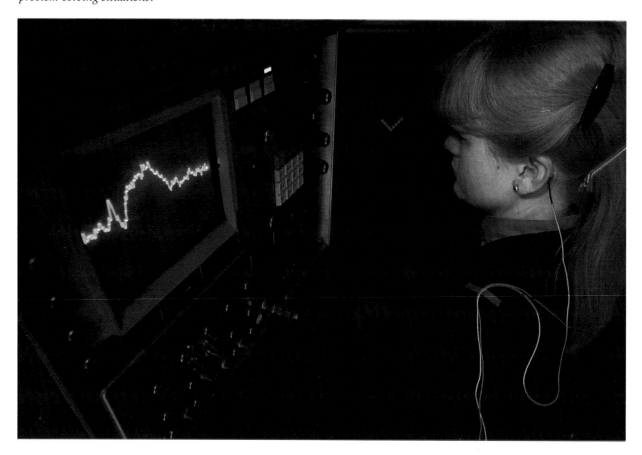

stereotype of creative individuals as odd, eccentric, neurotic, or even psychotic, and therefore totally out of touch with reality. Although examples can be found to fit such stereotypes (the artist Vincent van Gogh, perhaps), most evidence suggests that creative individuals are generally psychologically well-adjusted. Recent research, such as the work of the American psychologist Frank Barron, has shown that creative individuals may be distinguished by their persistence, high energy levels, self-confidence, independence of judgment, flexibility and openness to experience, and tolerance of ambiguity.

Creative individuals also tend to be more aware and more accepting of their own feelings, less bound by conventional sex role stereotypes, and more curious about their world than are less creative people. It has been suggested that although such characteristics may be genetically determined in the first instance, they are fostered by non-authoritarian parents, who encourage independence, and who are not overly concerned with neatness, obedience and emotional control.

Another popular fallacy that is inconsistent with the facts is that brilliant ideas and solutions to problems simply come to creative individuals in a flash of insight that occurs more or less by chance. Rather, it has been shown that creativity often depends on a highly cultivated mind and a sequence of complex mental tasks, from "preparation" to "revision," often taking place over a period of many years.

The question of what specific cognitive skills are necessary for creativity remains unanswered. It has been suggested that "divergent thinking," or the capacity to generate multiple solutions to a problem, might be the key to the creative process. This kind of thinking stands in contrast to "convergent thinking," which involves integrating information into a single solution. It is this kind of

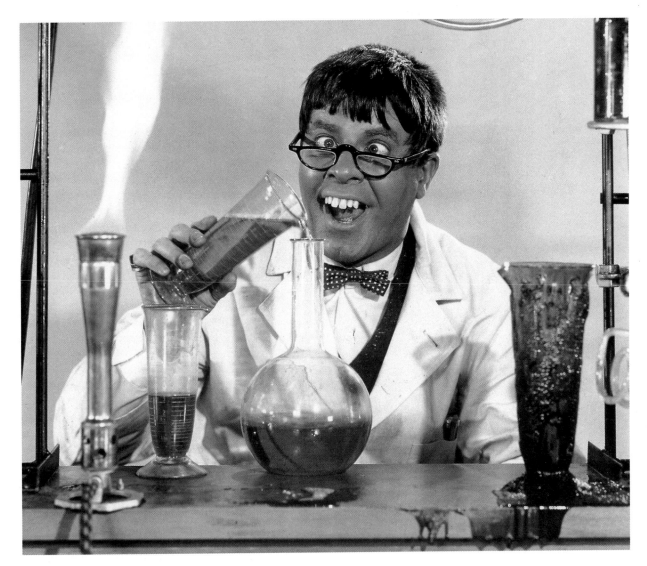

thinking that is assessed by most intelligence tests.
In fact, creativity probably requires both divergent
and convergent thinking.

The introspection of people regarded as creative
in various fields has given rise to suggestions that
certain basic mental processes underlie creativity.
These include the abilities to: form unusual associations, think "laterally," form visual images, use
metaphor, and relax conscious thought in order to
gain access to more primitive modes of thinking.
These tendencies may be likened to the kind of
thinking that often characterizes dreams, in which
images come and go in a nonlogical, non-
sequential fashion.

These suggestions are interesting in the light of
findings of different mental processses, or laterali-
zation of functioning, associated with each hemisphere of the brain. Sperry's studies of split-brain
patients who have undergone surgery to sever the
fibers connecting the hemispheres for the relief of

Actively participating, this baby enjoys a story read by mother. Children receiving preschool education are likely to display recognizable intellectual gains over other children when starting school.

epilepsy, have shown that the dominant (usually left) hemisphere controls the opposite (usually right) side of the body and is associated with verbal ability. The non-dominant (usually right) hemisphere controls the opposite (usually left) side of the body and is associated with spatial ability. It is possible that creative people are those who are able to switch more readily between the two different modes of thinking.

Shaping the Young Mind

Formal education is a deliberate effort to shape the mind through experience and to cause persistent behavior changes in the student. This directed effort to provide an optimal atmosphere for behavior change may be a special ability of the human species. In developed countries, the proportion of the day a child spends in school is considerable, especially between the ages of five and fifteen years. Attendance at school is neither compulsory nor typical in other parts of the world. A comparison of unschooled Mexican village children with their US counterparts showed that those with school experience had better strategies for solving cognitive problems. For example, by using "chunking" they could remember more items on a list seen for a short time then removed.

There is inevitably variety in the quality of schools and teachers: "She was a good teacher," "That was a poor school," "That textbook was useless," are typical teenage remarks. Research has shown that the most successful teacher is one who expects the student to do well and teaches basic skills in a structured manner. Pessimistic, critical teachers have much less effect on their pupils. The value of optimism and positive expectation seems especially important in the first year or two of school.

The principles of learning and memory are widely applied in educational practice. Instructional programs are targeted at attaining student competence in a new skill or way of thinking. Classroom tasks are designed to produce behavior change. Through such tasks, successful teachers can assess the students' current state of knowledge, correct errors or fill gaps in information, and guide them toward the next goal. For example, if a preschooler is being taught how to tie a shoe, the teacher must first teach him or her how to make a loop in one tie. The child is then allowed to try making the loop; the teacher then assesses the student's effort, gives feedback, and defines the next instructional step required to learn the new skill. This process is reminiscent of the shaping by successive approximation used in operant conditioning. The procedure also takes account of the memory constraints of the child and builds up retrieval pathways.

Some modern trends in education reflect efforts to apply learning theory in the teaching setting. One is the use of "mastery" courses, in which the objectives for each level are clearly specified to the teacher and student: "Today we will learn how to do long division." In some of the efforts at mastery teaching, students are able to pace themselves, possibly using computer-assisted programmed instruction or reinforcement by the teacher. These methods provide for an optimal amount of positive feedback toward acquiring new skills.

Another modern trend is to enlist the support of parents to help in teaching skills that are normally learned in school. In the Head Start program, referred to earlier in this chapter the children who were most successful academically were those for whom there was the most parental involvement in both instruction and encouragement.

Mainstreaming is a third modern trend in which children of all abilities and with all types of handicap are mixed within the same school setting. Blind or deaf children thus go to the school with their sighted and hearing peers. Ideally, this has the effect of making the disabled more used to a world filled with able-bodied people, and training able-bodied children to respect and cope with those who are less fortunate. If attention is paid to special needs within the mainstreaming scheme and preparation given for the social adjustment of everyone involved, then these ideals may be realized to some genuine degree.

A growing number of schools from the elementary right up to college level use computers as teaching aids. This method, sometimes called computer-assisted instruction, can reduce learning time and improve students' performances, particularly if it involves feedback between the machine and the student.

Chapter 4

A Meeting of Minds

When two people meet they can communicate in various ways. The most common is by speaking a language they both know. If, for any reason, either speaker has a speech or hearing problem, the two speakers can still communicate through nonverbal gestures of the face and body, which are otherwise important adjuncts to spoken conversation. This chapter describes some of what psychologists have learned about language in its "normal" form (that is, when the participants can speak and hear normally) and shows how the spoken message is augmented in other ways and by other means.

Language is the means by which we represent thought and communicate it to others. Species other than *Homo sapiens* have their own means of communication, and the distinguishing features of human language can thus be identified by considering and comparing the various methods of communication. For instance, a bee is able to communicate to other bees when it has found food. Having found food near to the hive, the bee dances in a circle when it returns to the hive. The richer the food source, the more vigorous and longer is the dance. This stimulates the other bees to seek out flowers with the same scent as carried by the bee that is performing the dance.

If the food source lies farther from the hive, the bee performs a different, figure-of-eight dance which indicates not only the type of flower that contains the food source but also where it can be found. In this case the bee wags its tail. The scent the returning bee carries again indicates to the other bees the type of flower they should seek. The distance and direction to the food are communicated by the tempo of the dance and the direction that the bee faces. The bee's dance is a means of communication, but it is very specific and, unlike human language, cannot be used for any other purpose. Also, it is instinctual and not adaptable, whereas our language has both these attributes. Birds also have a means of communicating with

Linguists have long sought to discover whether the present multiplicity of languages have a common origin, or whether they evolved separately. In the account given in the Biblical book Genesis, mankind was once blessed with a common tongue, but the willfulness of the Babylonians, who decided to build a tower that would reach up to heaven, provoked God's displeasure. To frustrate their purpose, He decides: "Come let us go down, and there confound their language, that they may not understand one another's speech." As shown in this detail from Pieter Breughel's painting, the tower remained unfinished, and the workers were scattered over the face of the Earth, each speaking a separate language (or "babbling").

89

each other which is unlike human language.

Birdsong is thus entirely different from the language of the bees in that it is not completely fixed in form. Nor is it like human language, because it does not allow a wide variety of messages to be communicated. The adaptability of birdsong may indicate why birds are often good mimics of, among other sounds, human voices. However, although such birds can reproduce the sound of a voice, they have no understanding of the meaning of the language itself (in spite of what proud owners might think). This demonstrates that producing something that is identifiable as speech is not in itself a sufficient basis for language.

There are essentially two sorts of birdsong — alarm calls, and songs produced during the breeding season to attract a mate. Woodland species have similar alarm calls. But the songs produced during the mating season differ quite markedly among various species, and even the same species in different areas may show subtly different "dialects."

Insects and birds are so different from humans, however, that it may be thought unreasonable to compare their means of communication to means as complex as ours. A closer examination of other species may reveal more similarities. Our nearest neighbors on the evolutionary tree are the higher apes, and for this reason researchers have investigated whether these animals can produce and understand human language.

Aping Humans

Several investigators have attempted to teach a language to chimpanzees. In an early attempt, in the United States in the 1950s, the Hayes family tried to teach English to a chimpanzee called Viki. The chimpanzee was brought up in their own household as if she were a child. After three years, Viki was able to say only three words: "Mama," "Papa," and "cup." Viki said "cup" when she wanted a drink, but "Mama" and "Papa" were not used appropriately. A five-year-old human child with normal intelligence, by comparison, has a vocabulary of several hundred words and a much higher level of proficiency in language.

It is possible, of course, that apes might be unable to produce speech even though they might

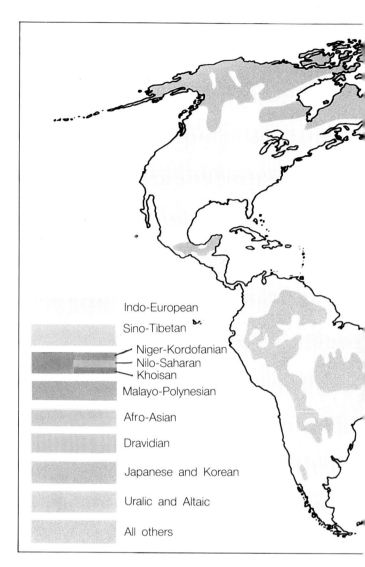

Indo-European

Sino-Tibetan

Niger-Kordofanian
Nilo-Saharan
Khoisan

Malayo-Polynesian

Afro-Asian

Dravidian

Japanese and Korean

Uralic and Altaic

All others

yet be able to understand language. It would then follow that if a chimpanzee was supplied with some other means by which to communicate its understanding, evidence for language comprehension would be obtained.

Suppose a child is born congenitally unable to speak but with perfectly good hearing and intelligence. The child would probably acquire a fair command of language but be unable to communicate by speaking. If the child was shown how to make use of some other means of communication, such as a typewriter or paper and pencil, he or she should be able to learn to use them in combination with the language to communicate with the outside world.

Such a case has been reported by Adrian Fourcin of University College, London, with a patient who is a congenital quadriplegic spastic. This patient was unable to communicate to any extent until he was provided with a foot-operated electric type-

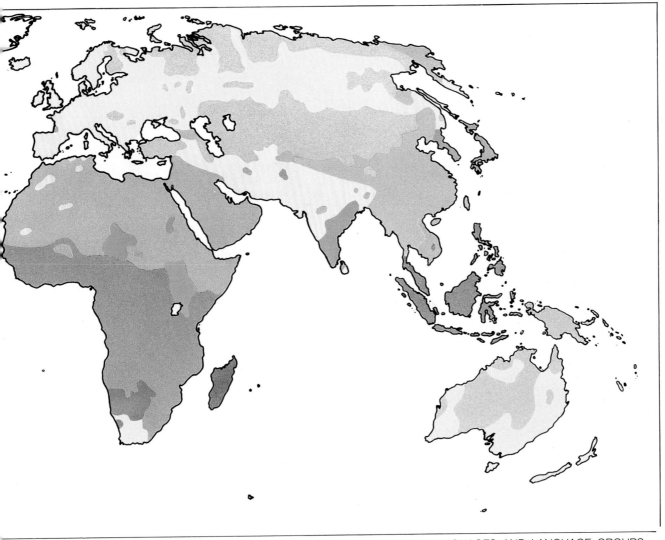

writer. Within nine days of receiving the type-writer, he wrote to the manufacturers to suggest an improvement in its design. This latent language-processing ability came as a big surprise, even to his parents. The patient has gone on to become a professionally qualified computer programmer. Thus, with the provision of an appropriate method of communication, he was able to show his understanding of language.

But to return to the capabilities of chimpanzees, the early researchers suspected that chimpanzees might be physically unable to produce human speech. Evidence has since come to light in support of their hunch. To understand it, knowing something about how speech is produced in humans is necessary.

Essentially, air is allowed to escape from the lungs through the vocal cords. As it does so it produces sound that is altered by the coordinated use of the tongue, the lips, the muscles of the

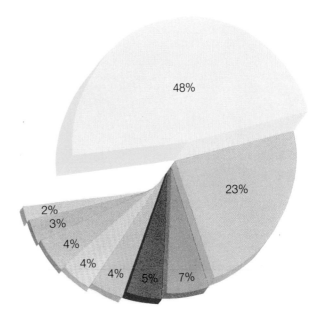

91

Human facial expressions resemble those of primates. Pleasure (A), concentration (B) and anger (C) produce similar expressions; but a "laughing" chimp (D), unlike a laughing man (E), is annoyed.

cheeks and the jaw — by themselves or in combination. This process, although it comes to be automatic in those with no physical disability, is complex; it is also very precise. Unless you hold your vocal apparatus in about the correct position, you cannot produce the correct sound.

You can try this out for yourself; say "ee" (as in "me") and hold your tongue in the position you used after you have completed it. Now, without moving your tongue, try to say "oo" (as in "moo"). You will find that the task is impossible: the position of the tongue is crucial in determining the vowel sound produced. If apes cannot produce the sounds of English, then might it be because they are not capable of positioning the tongue, lips and so on in the various positions used in the language?

Experimenters have found that it is possible to define all the possible positions of the vocal apparatus of humans or apes by making plaster casts.

Measurements made from the plaster casts can be entered into a computer program, and the sound that would emerge calculated. A playback of these sounds can then be used to determine which sounds the apes are capable of producing compared with those used in human languages.

Scientists who did this found that apes are incapable of producing the range of sounds produced in any human language. More recently, other scientists have determined that Neanderthal man could not produce all of the speech sounds used by present-day adults, and neither can newborn babies. Following birth, however, the vocal tracts of children alter quickly and they soon achieve the shape that allows them full speech.

Subsequent researchers with chimpanzees, who attributed their experimental results to the animals' inability to use our form of speech, searched for some other means of communication that they might be able to substitute. Two methods have been tried. American Sign Language was used by the Gardners with their chimpanzee Washoe.

As a result of training, Washoe eventually knew about five hundred signs; she could reliably use eighty of them. She was, however, able to generalize from the signs to related objects. For example, the sign for "dog" was learned by using a picture of a dog but was used spontaneously when she confronted a real dog. Washoe was thus able to demonstrate a much better grasp of communicating through language than Viki's when the problems involved in vocal communication were circumvented by using sign language.

The Premacks used colored symbols intended to stand for various objects with their chimpanzee called Sarah. Sarah showed a greater understanding of language than had Viki. In fact, she provided some evidence which might indicate that chimpanzees can use language to stand for items not present. Given the symbols for "Brown color of chocolate," Sarah selected a brown disk even though no chocolate was present. The results of experiments in which chimpanzees are given some way of representing language in a form other than speech show that they can use language with some facility. The consensus is, however, that the apes' use of human forms of language is rudimentary in comparison with our own. On the other hand, it is still perfectly possible that other species might have a means of communication as complex as that of humans. Whales, for example, are well known to have elaborate communication systems, but they have little in common with human languages.

The Asymmetric Brain

Parts of the human brain seem to be specialized for the production of language. Although it might be expected that each physically symmetrical half or hemisphere of the brain would have identical functions, it does not seem to be the case. The dominant, usually left, hemisphere is generally associated with language ability, whereas the non-dominant, usually right, hemisphere is associated with visuospatial ability. Areas of the brain are also associated with specific mental functions. In the nineteenth century, the celebrated French anatomist and anthropologist Pierre Paul Broca investigated the brain of a man who was unable to speak.

Different systems of animal communication have come under increasingly close scrutiny because they may provide clues to the workings of human language. Dolphins, with their large brains and extensive vocabulary of clicks and whistles, have been obvious candidates for research. In one series of experiments, a dolphin that had been taught a specific trick was placed in a tank beside that of a "novice" dolphin which could hear it but not see it. In almost every case, the novice dolphin learned the same trick in a shorter period of time, presumably through following signals communicated by its companion.

He found that tissue was missing in the anterior speech region of the frontal lobe, and concluded that the lack of this area of the brain was directly responsible for the patient's loss of expressive speech. Subsequent work has supported Broca's observation, and this part of the brain is now called Broca's area in his honor.

Other parts of the brain have also been found to be important in language function. Patients with damage in the location known as Wernicke's area are still physically able to produce speech, but they have difficulty understanding language. The function attributed to this part of the brain is receptive speech. Thus, when this area is damaged, the associations are scrambled and become interpreted by the hearer as meaningless messages.

Making Sense of What We Hear

There is another significant aspect of speech — its sensory perception. It is important first to determine whether other species are capable of perceiving the sounds of our language in the same way as we do. Obviously, if a species were physically incapable of perceiving our language, then the members would not be able to demonstrate that they understood it. Yet, at the same time, if animals are not able to hear the differences between sounds (as deaf people cannot), this does not necessarily mean that they are incapable of understanding language.

The unit sounds that are used in a language spoken by humans are called phonemes. These correspond approximately to the consonants and vowels of writing; they may not correspond to the spelling because English (like most languages) is not spelled particularly closely to the way it is pronounced. Many words have changed their pronunciation over time without corresponding changes in the spelling. Language can be perceived if a listener is able to determine the composition and sequence of phonemes a word contains. The word "pet" for example, contains a "p," an "e" and a "t" in that order. The sound associated with a "p" in English varies as a function of a number of factors (such as the sounds either side of it), as do the sounds of virtually all the other English phonemes. However, listeners do not usually notice these differences; instead they re-

94

spond to all the different instances of "p" as belonging to the same category.

This ability, to respond to the category a sound belongs to rather than to the subtler acoustic differences, is called "categorical perception." Much like adults, infants as young as six months of age respond to these sounds in this way. This has been demonstrated in the following way. To find out whether babies respond to the distinction between the two related sounds "b" and "p," a nipple is placed in a baby's mouth. The baby commences sucking but receives no food. At the same time as the nipple is placed in the baby's mouth, a speech sound (say a syllable beginning with "b") is played repeatedly. Eventually the baby stops sucking on the nipple. When the experimenter observes that the sucking rate has dropped, he or she alters the sound. If the sound changes — for example, from a syllable with an initial "b" to a syllable with an initial "p" — the baby's sucking rate increases once more. But, if the sound alters from a "b" to another "b" (which may be just as different as the "b" and "p" in terms of

its other sound properties), no increase in sucking rate occurs.

One possible interpretation of these findings is that the ability to respond categorically is innate. In fact, chinchillas have been shown to respond to sounds categorically. Thus, it seems that at least some other mammals respond categorically to speech sounds. This may be because these species have auditory systems like our own, which are able to perceive the sounds used for speech.

How is it that two speech sounds can differ and yet still be recognizable as the same word? After all, women and children have voices pitched higher than adult males. Although the voices sound different, the human brain seems able to identify different speech sounds as being the same words. Another difference is accent. Many people can identify what part of the country a strange-sounding speaker comes from, but the unfamiliar pronunciation does not necessarily cause any particular problems in comprehending what he or she is saying.

Sounds spoken even by the same speaker can

differ in different speaking contexts. If you speak fast for example, many sounds alter in their properties. Speakers generally have the impression that they are producing separate words, as if the words "pop out" of the speech — but if sounds of speech are examined, they are likely to be perceived as running into each other. Consider the words "big gate," for example: you may think, on reading the words, that you pronounce both the "g"'s (one at the end of "big" and one at the start of "gate") — but if you listen carefully to yourself or a friend saying the words, you should notice that although the timing is slowed enough for two consonants, there is only one "g" actually pronounced.

Some phrases also illustrate this point. If you say the once-popular nursery rhyme "Mares eat oats and does eat oats and little lambs eat ivy, a kid'll eat ivy too — wouldn't you?", you may find that listeners have difficulty separating out the words so that the meaning can be understood. All of these factors make it difficult to write a successful computer program for voice analysis of direct speech in order to convert it into (say) written form. Some advances have been made, but there is still a long way to go.

Speaking in Tongues

Many languages other than English do not include English phonemes, so that speakers who try to learn English (even after years of trying) may never learn how to produce the sounds we use. One example is Japanese. Most Japanese find it difficult to distinguish between "r"'s and "l"'s, and comedians often imitate Japanese accents by exchanging these two sounds. On the other hand, almost all other languages use sounds that we do not; a number use different conventions in pronunciation altogether. Chinese is an example. To Western ears Chinese speech has a "sing-song" sound. This is produced by altering voice pitch

(intonation) in a precisely controlled manner. So in Chinese, a word spoken with a rising pitch means one thing, while the same word uttered with a falling pitch means another. In English, intonation is not used in such a precise way although it does have some linguistic significance.

Nonverbal Communications

There is more to communicating through language than simply producing speech. A speaker can adopt different postures, and move his or her hands to emphasize different aspects of the message. Such body postures can be used for communication even in the absence of speech; they may be used intentionally — such as a shrug of the shoulders — or the communicator might not be aware of them. These gestures, in all their forms, are means of nonverbal communication.

Several questions about nonverbal communication have been considered by psychologists, but two are of particular interest. First is the question of whether this form of communication has its basis in our animal forebears. Second, there is the question of whether people from different cultures show similar characteristics in their means of communicating nonverbally.

It has been convincingly demonstrated that much in the behavior of animals consists of communication by nonverbal signs. These include obvious visual indications such as sexual readiness; for example, some female primates signal this by blue swellings on their buttocks. Other aspects are more subtle. The order of authority among different apes in a group is signaled by strictly defined protocols. Now that these methods of communication in animals have been identified, scientists are trying to relate them to the behavior of, for instance, a man looking for a sexual partner. If a connection could be demonstrated, then it may be that such behavior has its origins remote in our evolutionary past.

The investigation of whether nonverbal communication signals are universal could be used to improve communication between people from different countries. If a businessman wants to make a deal, it is important for him to be aware of whether the nonverbal communication signals which are polite in his own culture are in the other one. For

The "eyebrow flash," in which the eyebrows are raised to their full extent for about one-sixth of a second, is recognized instinctively the world over as a gesture of surprise or, among couples, as one of flirtatiousness. Marlene Dietrich removed her natural eyebrows and used cosmetics to achieve the same expression permanently — perhaps a contributory factor in the enormous attraction of her sultry image.

earlier. It is sometimes used for linguistic purposes; at other times, it is used to convey emphasis or emotion. For example, particular intonations indicate that a statement is made angrily or with a hint of sarcasm.

Pitch of the voice is also an important clue in dialogue as to the definition of a conclusion. Typically, when a speaker has finished what he or she wants to say, pitch drops. Other nonverbal communicative signals also contribute, such as looks and gestures. Psychologist Geoff Beatty from Sheffield University, England, noted that Prime Minister Margaret Thatcher often seemed to be interrupted by interviewers. When he analyzed her intonation, looks and gazes, he observed that she appeared to be indicating that she had finished her turn, at which time the interviewer naturally took up the conversation. Often, however, she had not, and when she continued speaking, it appeared to the audience that the interviewer was constantly interrupting.

Semantics and Syntax

The brain is also involved in producing the grammatically correct sentences of languages. What is meant by a language is a (possibly infinite) set of sentences. Syntax regulates the proper sequence of ideas expressed in the sentences, and grammar tells us what is permissible in the form of the words in the sentences. Grammar does not indicate whether a sentence is meaningful or not, only whether it conforms to the rules of form. A sentence such as "The wind killed a book" is thus grammatically correct but meaningless. Interpretation of meaning falls within the competence of the branch of linguistics called semantics.

It is not necessary to evaluate the accuracy of a sentence in order to establish whether it conforms to the rules of our language. This, and other, observations about language convinced the celebrated American linguist Noam Chomsky that the process of learning a language is not simply a matter of learning by association (as a dog might learn to associate the sound of a bell with the arrival of food). Rather, Chomsky argues, we are endowed with an innate ability to learn the rules of syntax and grammar in our own language. Thus, when faced with a novel sentence, we can apply

example, most English-speaking people regard direct looks into the face as threatening, and it is customary for a speaker who does not wish to appear aggressive to avert his or her gaze. In Greece, however, it is normal to stare directly in the face. When confronted with English speakers, Greeks often feel that they are being ignored. If the businessman is aware of this, he may be able to overcome this cultural clash and take steps to avoid jeopardizing his deal.

There are certain nonverbal communication signals, such as facial expressions that reveal emotions, that do seem to be universal. They are also found in deaf and blind children, who could not have learned them by imitation. One example is the "eye-brow flash," used extensively in flirting, in which the eyebrows are raised to their full extent for about one-sixth of a second. Humans also use aspects of the voice as a means of signaling their feelings. Voice pitch was mentioned

Touching gives expression to feelings and establishes relationships with others. A 1966 American study showed, in terms of percentages, where male and female students most often made contact with parents (the pale figures) and with friends of the same and the opposite sex. Mothers, for example, touched their daughters' arms 76 to 100 per cent of the time, whereas with their sons hand contact was most frequent.

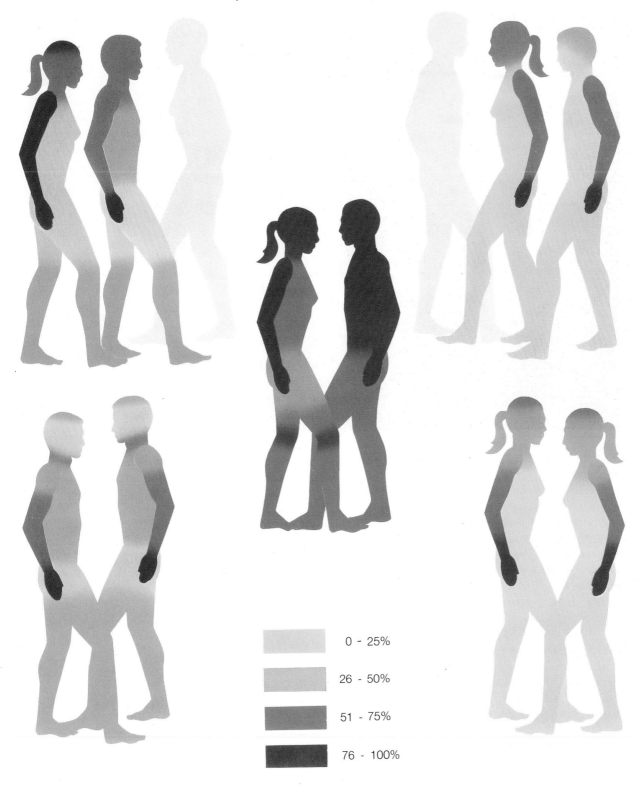

	0 - 25%
	26 - 50%
	51 - 75%
	76 - 100%

the rules; we do not need to have had any previous experience of it or even sentences like it.

To explain more fully the essence of Chomsky's views, first consider parsing — breaking a sentence down into its component words. At school, children used to learn that words can be characterized as nouns, adjectives, verbs and so on. These components could be further categorized so that, for example, a noun could be the subject or object of a sentence. The components of any sentence could be labeled in this way; thus:

The boy read a book.
could be categorized as:

Article + Noun + Verb + Article + Noun
simply from the definition of these units. If a noun phrase is defined as "Article + Noun," it could also be written:

Noun phrase + Verb + Noun Phrase.
This analysis tells us that other sentences such as

A farmer killed the cow

has exactly the same structure. Parsing — like grammar in general — does not offer a prescription as to whether a sentence is meaningful or not. Meaningless sentences may, after all, have this same structure.

The next step is to formulate syntactical and grammatical rules. Three simple rules might read something like "A sentence consists of, at least, a noun phrase plus a verb phrase" (rule 1); "A verb phrase consists of, at least, a verb plus a noun phrase" (rule 2); and "A noun phrase consists of, at least, an article plus a noun" (rule 3). These can be represented symbolically as follows:

Rule 1: $S \rightarrow NP + VP$
Rule 2: $VP \rightarrow V + NP$
Rule 3: $NP \rightarrow Art + N$

where the symbol S stands for "sentence," NP for "noun phrase," VP for "verb phrase," V for "verb," Art for "article" and N for "noun."

If we now start again with our original sentence,

"The boy read a book," rule 3 tells us that we can write "NP" every time we see an article plus a noun. So if we did this, we would get "NP + read + NP," since "the boy" and "a book" both consist of an article plus a noun. Rule 2 indicates that every time a verb plus a noun phrase occurs, a verb phrase exists. Thus now the sentence is "NP + VP" because "read + NP" is a verb followed by a noun phrase. Finally, rule 1 states that a sentence consists of a noun phrase plus verb phrase (which is exactly what we have), so according to these rules this is a syntactically correct sentence.

To verify whether it is also grammatically correct, we need check only that the form of the verb corresponds in number with its subject, as do the articles with their respective nouns. These rules are extremely simple, but they serve to illustrate the idea. The concept of "subject" and "object" is thus important. Virtually always in English, although not necessarily in other languages (such

Following wild reindeer through a landscape that remains wintry nine months of the year, the Lapps of northern Europe have a large store of words to express subtle changes in the texture of what most Northerners refer to simply as one word: "snow." The English language has, however, incorporated at least one Lapp word — tundra — meaning "high place where nothing grows."

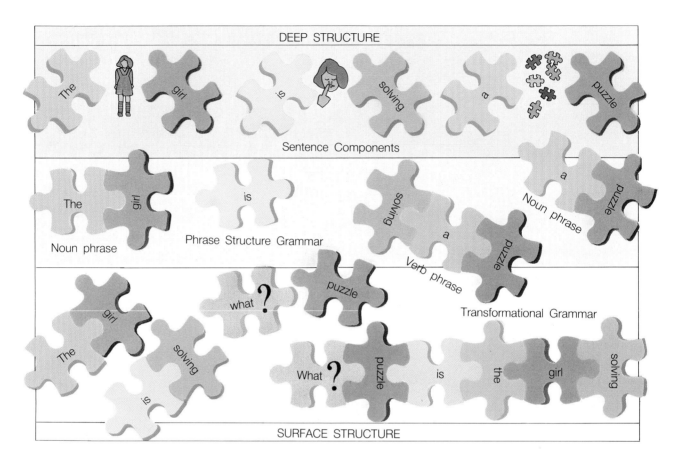

DEEP STRUCTURE

Sentence Components

Phrase Structure Grammar

Noun phrase

Transformational Grammar

Verb phrase

SURFACE STRUCTURE

Although some linguists are unconvinced that an aptitude for forming meaningful grammatical structures is inborn, the complexity of the process lends itself to a more sophisticated model than the merely associative. Traditional grammar parses a sentence into word-units and combinations of word-units, but is not concerned with the relationship between a statement and its conversion into a question. Transformational rules apply specifically to this, distinguishing between the "deep structure" of the root sentence and the "surface structure" of its realization, and suggesting a possibly innate ability to make the leap from one to the other.

as Hebrew), the first noun phrase expressed is the subject and the noun phrase that follows the verb is the object. English sentences thus generally follow the structure "subject verb object" (usually abbreviated S V O).

The system of characterizing sentences according to the nature of their constituent units is called phrase structure grammar. Phrase structure grammar uses transformational rules to enable a sentence such as "The boy is reading a book" to be transformed into sentences like "What book is the boy reading?" The first sentence could be rewritten without requiring much modification of the original rules as "The boy is reading what book?" All that has been done which was not included in the earlier rules is that the interrogative adjective "what" has been substituted for the article.

To derive the second sentence, however, transformational rules are needed. The first rule is to move "what book" to the beginning of the sent-

102

ence. When this is done, the sentence obtained is:

What book the boy is reading + O.

("O" stands for the gap left by moving "what book".) The next transformational rule is to invert the subject ("the boy") and the auxiliary verb ("is") to give:

What book is the boy + O + reading + O

(The first "O" indicates the gap left by moving "is".) This example illustrates that the second sentence can be formed from the first by application of these two transformational rules.

The transformational rules are called, respectively, "Wh-fronting" and "Aux-inversion" (standing for auxiliary inversion). The first rule is called Wh-fronting rather than "What-fronting" because it also applies to other interrogative adjectives, such as "who," "where," "when," "which" and "why." The first type of sentence, inasmuch as it represents the fundamental structure, is often referred to as the root sentence.

Chomsky's emphasis on the importance of grammatical transformations in language has had a powerful impact on the thinking of linguists, whether they agree with his views or not. In addition his theories have significance for the psychologist interested in language. First, Chomsky emphasizes the rule-governed nature of language. Second, the rules of language may be innately endowed.

This brief consideration of some aspects of human communication indicates the complexity of language systems. Much of our understanding about language is now being used in order to permit machines to be able to produce speech. Some progress has been made in this direction already. Machines will soon be commercially available that can take a printed page of text from a book, optically scan the page, and convert it to spoken output, a technique of enormous potential benefit to blind people.

Chapter 5

The Hidden Self

To "know oneself" has become a modern preoccupation, but the quest to uncover and control the hidden reasons for our behavior has been a long one. The result is a bewildering array of techniques assembed over millennia that profess to reveal these secrets, and it is hard for an ordinary person to judge the powerful claims made for them. However, since the opening years of this century, researchers have turned the principal weapons of science onto the dark fortress of human motivation. Some of the secrets are already disclosed. In the process, scientists have come to understand what techniques such as meditation, biofeedback and psychoanalysis may offer to the search for self knowledge.

One source of resistance had to be overcome before the scientists' onslaught could begin. Some people felt that the notion of a "secret mind" was an insult to the human race. Humans were, so they argued, rational creatures, aware of all the forces affecting behavior, thoughts and feelings. A critical modern blow to this view was dealt by the writings, not of a laboratory scientist, but of a doctor who practiced in Vienna from 1886 to 1938.

Sigmund Freud found it hard to accept the explanation for his patients' symptoms that was handed down to him by his teachers. He was told that these bizarre symptoms (which would now be described as neurotic) were conscious and calculated attempts by the patients to seek attention. By listening carefully to what his patients said to him, Freud came to realize that they were tormented by their symptoms. They were victims of forces quite beyond their control. The forces, although present in everyone, were totally hidden from view, arising from deep below the level of consciousness. Freud thought that the most powerful of these forces were sexual motivation and aggression, and he called them the "life and death instincts." Freud drew his conclusions from the close observation of phenomena in many patients over a period of years, and his glimpses behind the walls

The mask of Janus symbolizes the two opposing sides of human personality. One face looks outward joyously, the other seems inwardly-turned and is full of despair. Janus was the Roman god of gates and entrances, and kept watch in both directions. His favor was invoked at the start of any major undertaking because he was said also to look into the past and into the future. Similar two-faced deities are found in other cultures — duality is a universal theme of human mind and existence.

of the unconscious helped the army of scientists who followed to aim their attack more keenly.

Aggression in Humans

In describing aggression as an instinct, Freud in later years was pessimistic about the prospects for his species. Firstly, he argued that an instinct was inborn and therefore could not be much modified by upbringing. Secondly, it carried an energy of its own which built up until it could not be contained. When the conflict between containment, or repression, and expression was sufficient, it resulted in aggressive discharge. Freud gloomily wrote in the early 1930s, as he watched European nations prepare for World War II, "The death instinct turns into the destructive instinct . . . The living creature preserves its own life . . . by destroying an extraneous one."

Working in Germany, thirty years after Freud's death, the natural scientist Konrad Lorenz began painting a more optimistic, conservative picture of the aggression instinct. He described how, even in lower animals, naked aggression is rarely seen. Most "battles" are no more than rituals of threat and counterthreat in which the weaker party is made to retreat and give way, usually without violence or injury. For example, the impressive and menacing antlers of the deer are used for just that purpose — impressing an opponent in a

fighting "ritual." This may entail entangling antlers for a while, but each animal follows intricate "rules" so as to avoid serious injury to the other. The task for mankind, according to Lorenz, is to learn to use this sort of harmless ritual to discharge aggression. Lorenz himself advocated sports as an effective "safety valve."

These are important claims and stimulated researchers to find out whether giving people an opportunity to be aggressive does, as Lorenz promised, leave them less aggressive for a while. From kindergarten children to adults, the answer appears to be the same; aggression fosters further aggression. The dreadful results of this process taken to its extreme can be seen in the brutality of war. And it seems that seeing other people behave aggressively on a television screen, even in a fictional context, can have the same effect.

Discoveries about the way in which the brain controls aggression also qualified the role of instinct. By using a small electric current passed through a fine wire into a specific part of an animal's brain, scientists can stimulate the nerve cells there into activity, and watch the result on the animal's behavior. In this way it was found that the areas controlling aggression lay deep in the limbic system, a part of the brain which has long been known to be crucial in motivation. When one scientist went on to study in more detail the effects

Aggression (left) appears to be an emotion that lies deep in all people, a remnant from humankind's remote past. In part, it still acts as a spur to constructive action, but it also produces violence, crime and war.

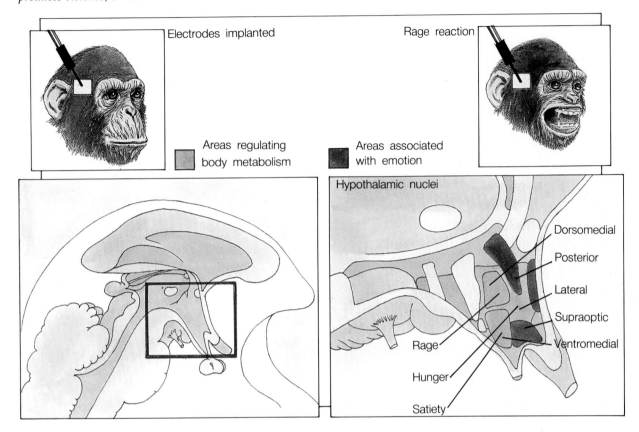

Electrodes implanted

Rage reaction

Areas regulating body metabolism

Areas associated with emotion

Hypothalamic nuclei

Dorsomedial
Posterior
Lateral
Supraoptic
Ventromedial

Rage
Hunger
Satiety

of stimulating one part of this system in monkeys, his results revealed much about aggression.

To understand these results it is necessary to know one crucial fact about monkeys' social life. When a group is formed, a "ranking" quickly emerges; one monkey becomes the "dominant" animal, and the others take up more and more subordinate positions. If the hypothalamus of a dominant monkey was stimulated, it attacked any of the subordinate males which it could reach — although it scrupulously avoided the females. If, however, a subordinate monkey was stimulated, it behaved differently. Instead of showing aggression, it showed fear, running away and cowering from the others.

The explanation is as follows. By stimulating the limbic system, aggression-provoking stimuli produce an unpleasant emotional feeling. (In this case the stimulus was electrical; in daily life it can be any unpleasant or frustrating act, such as being thwarted — beaten to something we wanted by

Probing with microscopic electrodes, researchers have located specific areas within the hypothalamus of the brain that play a large part in governing particular emotions. Other areas regulate certain body functions by stimulating the production of hormones. A rage reaction in a chimpanzee is induced when the dorsomedial nucleus is stimulated by a small electric current from the implanted electrode. When the current is turned off, the ape reverts to normal behavior. Similar results have been observed with humans, but further research has shown that other brain areas are also involved in emotional reactions.

In the animal kingdom, the strongest, healthiest individuals are those most likely to find a mate and succeed in bringing up offspring. A similar rule applies to human beings, but cultural influences have a modifying effect. In all societies, body image as well as social and economic status are important in attracting the opposite sex. Not everyone is a film star, but a great many people try to look and dress as if they were.

someone else or by our own incompetence.) Whether such a state leads us to "fight or flight" depends on the conditions. If it would be pointless or dangerous to fight — or if experience has taught that it would not be appropriate — we may choose to flee or to back down.

Sexual Behavior

Turning to the second of Freud's instincts, it has become clear that patterns of human sexual activity also owe much less to internal forces than to social ones. In the United States, attitudes to sexual activities have changed dramatically in the past half century. When Alfred Kinsey surveyed college-educated Americans in the 1940s, half the males had experienced premarital intercourse and only one-quarter of the females. In the 1980s, it is more than three-quarters of males and more than one-half of females.

Superimposed on these cultural effects there are some other internal influences, but they are weak by comparison. They arise from the sex hormones — substances produced by the testes in the male and the ovaries in the female — which

are carried in the blood to the brain where they can influence the way it responds to sexual stimuli. Normally, levels of the male hormones (or androgens) have little effect on sexual behavior. Castration, however, removes their source and decreases desire — although less in man than in other species.

The female sex hormones (or estrogens) are relatively unimportant in stimulating sexuality — when their release ceases with the menopause there is no great decline in sexual interest — but they do have a slight effect. The frequency with which women themselves initiate intercourse — or engage alone in sexual fantasy or self-stimulation — has been found to increase around the middle of the menstrual cycle, when estrogen levels are at their peak. By contrast, the females of other species generally engage in sexual behavior only during this period of "estrus" or "heat."

The Pangs of Hunger

The progress of evolution has released human beings from rigid control of sexual interest by internal factors in the way seen in less highly

evolved species. Variations in human aggressiveness, too, are dependent more on outside factors
than internal ones. But what of a third sort of
motivation — that which drives us to eat?

As might be expected, this motivation is, above
all others, closely controlled by bodily needs. The
control-house, once again, lies in a part of the
limbic system of the brain: the hypothalamus. One
part, the lateral hypothalamus, is the "eating center"; stimulating it with a minute electric current
drives an animal to eat — even if it is already
sated. Close by lies the ventromedial hypothalamus, which has the opposite function — it is a
"satiety center." Stimulation of this area stops a
hungry animal from eating. Occasionally, this part
of the brain, and the satiety signals which come
from it, is destroyed by a tumor; overeating and
obesity are the result.

The natural triggers that excite these groups of
brain cells are complex. In the very short term,
there are signals that reach the brain from the
stomach, telling it how full the stomach is. As a
person eats the stomach wall stretches, decreasing
electrical activity in the lateral hypothalamus, but
exciting that in the ventromedial part; this switches off eating. Other signals tell the hypothalamus
about current levels of blood sugar; increases have
the same effects as stretching of the stomach wall,
decreases the opposite. Despite short-term fluctua-
tions in energy needs, most animals and people
can balance food intake to keep their weight within
close limits over periods of years. This implies that
the hypothalamus must be responding too to an
index — at present unclear — of the body's long-
term state of nourishment or reserves.

Even in hunger, internal forces make up only
half the picture. To understand why food intake
may go awry, it is necessary also to consider
external influences on eating. In one experiment,
dogs could be persuaded to eat much more than
usual — and much more than they needed — by a
simple maneuver: at a number of stages during
their meal, the taste of the food of some was
changed while its identical nutritional value remained constant. So, faced with a dinner guest
sated on one course, simply bring on the next;
fresh appetite is aroused by the change in taste.

Sated animals can also be tricked into eating by a

Some people eat to live, others live to eat. Appetite is regulated by centers in the hypothalamus and other parts of the brain, and a healthy adult naturally eats the types and amounts of food he or she requires. When an individual overeats (or eats too little, as in those who suffer from anexoria nervosa), factors such as self-image, economic status, occupation and mental well-being are often involved.

That one emotion affects another is a common human experience. It is not a coincidence that an unhurried meal is often associated with romance. Conversely, some people find their appetite diminishes when in love.

second method. "Priming" them by putting a small amount of the food into their mouths may stimulate them to take more food. One early American psychologist dubbed this the "salted peanut phenomenon" — eat one and you want more. The food need not even be tasted for people to be successfully "primed." The sight or smell of food alone can create an appetite in most people.

A few people are especially sensitive to these appetite-enhancing ploys; if they are to avoid obesity, they have to struggle hard to restrain their eating. Even those who are successful at keeping their weight down to normal by reducing may eat more than normal eaters when they are given a mouth-watering description of the food which is tempting them. Their restraint is fragile and easily broken down by just those techniques which are exploited so well in our very culinary culture.

Arousal and the Emotions

It may seem odd that the arousal of anxiety should evoke quite a different motivation, such as the motivation to eat, but this is not an isolated occurrence. Aggressive impulses can give rise to fear, depending on the circumstances, and sexual arousal can turn to aggression or anger. In one experiment, being shown a pornographic movie made men become even angrier with someone who annoyed them immediately afterward. Even more curiously, after men have undergone strenuous physical exercise, they may also become angrier or, if they have been enjoying the company of a pretty girl, they may feel more sexually attracted to her.

Physical arousal is the key to understanding this fickle quality of motivation. To grasp this concept, the focus has to be shifted from the forces or drive states, such as hunger, which rise up from inside us, to the states, such as appetite, which are produced inside us by external stimuli. It is these influences, known colloquially and scientifically as "emotions," which are so important in steering human motivation.

Just as Sigmund Freud revealed the secrets of unconscious motivation, it was William James, an American philosopher, who at the turn of the last century did the same for emotions. His radical suggestion was that the processes which are important in shaping emotions are normally hidden from us. James thought that emotions are merely "snapshots" of our bodies' reactions. He gave this example: suppose you are out walking in the forest and you see a bear; you feel frightened and your body becomes aroused. Your heart beats faster and more powerfully, your hair stands on end, you perspire more heavily — you may well run away. The "commonsense" explanation is that seeing the bear causes fear, which in turn causes that arousal. James said that seeing the bear caused the arousal directly and that this state was viewed by the conscious mind as a feeling of fear.

Like Freud, James left his claim at the level of theory — untested by experimentation. Gradually, however, evidence has accumulated. For instance, his theory helps to explain how it is that patients who suffer accidental spinal damage feel less intense emotional experiences than they did before their injury. The spinal cord is the highway for information to the brain, telling it what is happening in the rest of the body; the accident cuts

The hypothalamus is a major link between the brain and the body's endocrine system (below). In response to the levels of sugars and hormones detected in the blood, it activates the pituitary to release hormones which, in turn, stimulate the other glands into hormone secretion. Shown on the right of the diagram is the body's reaction to stress or danger. Signals from the cerebral cortex cause the hypothalamus to stimulate the pituitary to release ACTH (adrenocorticotropic hormone). ACTH causes the adrenal glands to produce epinephrine and corticoid hormones, which speed up the body's metabolism of food chemicals.

THE ENDOCRINE SYSTEM

THE STRESS RESPONSE

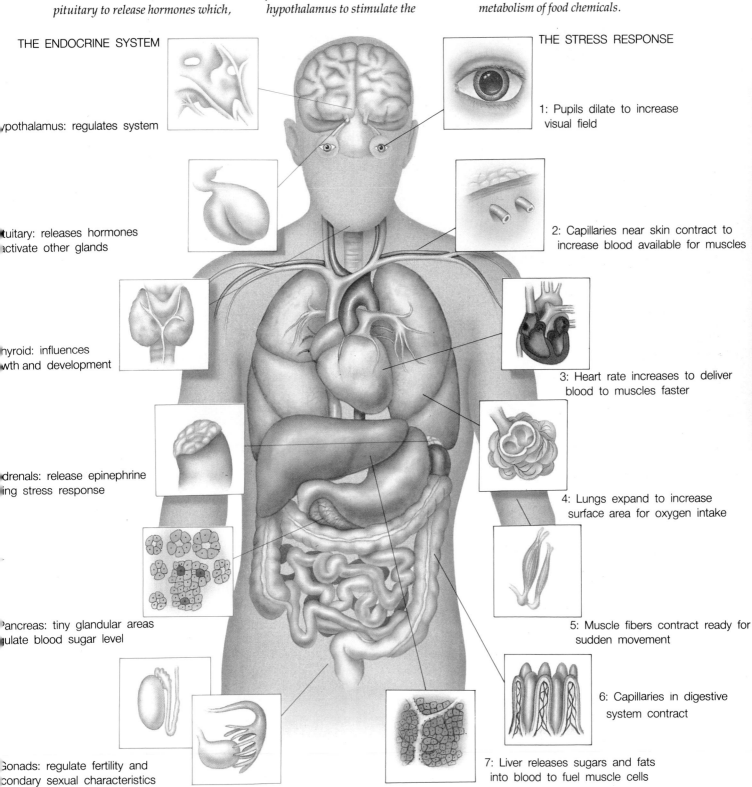

pothalamus: regulates system

1: Pupils dilate to increase visual field

tuitary: releases hormones activate other glands

2: Capillaries near skin contract to increase blood available for muscles

hyroid: influences wth and development

3: Heart rate increases to deliver blood to muscles faster

drenals: release epinephrine ing stress response

4: Lungs expand to increase surface area for oxygen intake

ancreas: tiny glandular areas gulate blood sugar level

5: Muscle fibers contract ready for sudden movement

6: Capillaries in digestive system contract

Gonads: regulate fertility and condary sexual characteristics

7: Liver releases sugars and fats into blood to fuel muscle cells

111

The extent and ease of human emotional arousal depends upon the situation and the individuals concerned. Some people have a ''short fuse'' and become angry at the smallest inconvenience, others may

be placid to the point that it seems as if they are almost incapable of emotion. On one occasion, haggling over the price of something in a sale may be enjoyable, on another it may lead to confrontation. Similarly, the

soaring downtown office blocks of a big city can inspire feelings of elation and excitement in someone already happy, while only adding to the loneliness of someone suffering from anxiety or depression.

the brain off from much of that information. The brain therefore ''thinks'' that the body has become less aroused, so less emotion is felt. This also makes it easy to understand how the arousal of one motivation so often stimulates another. An erotic film may produce arousal which can add to an arousal afterward by different motivation.

The work of an American psychologist, Stanley Schachter, has revealed much more about the way in which arousal is translated into a particular emotion. He thought that our experience of emotion depends on the attributions we make from the surrounding circumstances. To demonstrate this process, Schachter evoked emotional response in a group of college students, not by exposing them to an exciting event, but by an injection of the hormone epinephrine. This ''flight or fight'' hormone is normally released into the blood by the adrenal glands, and it arouses the body by stimulating organs such as the heart into greater activity. After

the injection — and without being told by Schachter what was happening — each student then went into another room. There, with the extra epinephrine in the bloodstream, they felt more emotional than did others who had gone through exactly the same procedure, but without receiving any extra epinephrine. The particular type of emotion they subsequently felt was determined by what was going on in the room into which they had been led. Some had the company of an actor pretending to be angry about what was going on; they became more angry. Others, placed with a ''happy'' actor, who was telling jokes, became even happier as a result of the injection.

Further, the extra emotional effect of the epinephrine was totally lost if the students were first told about its arousing effect. The implications of these results is that, when in a state of arousal, we automatically ''look around'' for the most plausible explanation. If we know that we have

Events that bring about a major change in a person's life are stressful for everyone. Marriage, parenthood, changes at work, or bereavement may trigger psychological problems in susceptible individuals.

just been injected with an arousing drug, that is sufficient; if we do not, we make the best judgment we can based on the evidence of what we see going on around us.

That this process lays people open to distortion is of tremendous importance in the psychiatric clinic. Some people experience occasional episodes of bodily arousal, lasting from a few minutes to an hour or two. It may sometimes be a result of non-serious heart disorder, or of stress or hormonal disturbance — after childbirth, for example — but the real reason is rarely clear to the sufferer. The experience leads, as Schachter has shown us, to a search for an explanation. Often, the explanation adopted is one of illness. The person may conclude, quite wrongly, that he or she has serious heart disease. This conclusion itself produces further stress, and makes a further attack even more likely. A painful vicious circle has been set up and, for example, the person may eventually be unable to venture far from home for fear of collapsing without anyone to help. What has been described is the development of agoraphobia, the fear of leaving the safety of home.

Observers of Our Own Actions

William James suggested that we infer our feelings from our bodies' muscular responses: we run away, so we feel afraid. Just as Schachter helped to clarify the role of arousal, another American psychologist, Daryl Bem, did the same for overt behavior. His view was this: when we observe ourselves behaving in a certain way toward an object — or, for that matter, a person or a political stance — we automatically seek explanations for our actions. Sometimes we find a reason in the outside — someone is paying us well to do so, for example. Sometimes, though, no such reason can be found. Instead we presume some internal one: "We are behaving this way because it reflects our feelings." If people find insufficient explanation around them for their actions, their feelings change to help explain what they have done.

Mistakes in the way people explain their own behavior often surface in a psychiatric clinic. Consider three events which happened to one young woman, still in her twenties but with a good managerial post in a leading company, during the

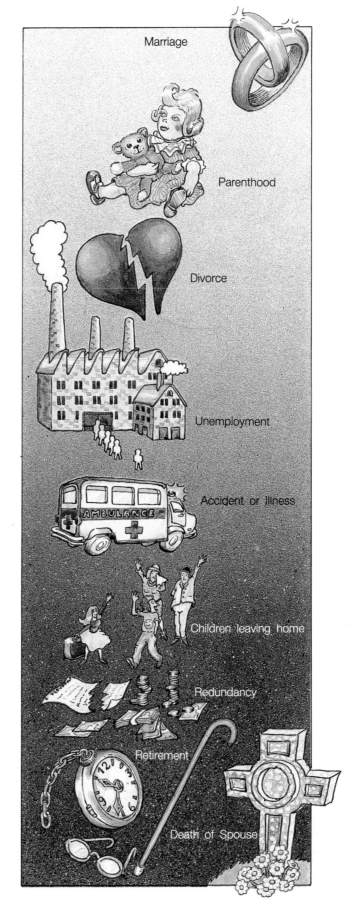

Marriage

Parenthood

Divorce

Unemployment

Accident or Illness

Children leaving home

Redundancy

Retirement

Death of Spouse

Studies into the psyche show that looking on the bright side is good psychological advice. People who label themselves as lonely or unhappy, often with no good reason, are more likely to suffer from prolonged depression than those with a more positive attitude. By concentrating on the better aspects of themselves and their lives for a period each day, such people can recover a sense of fulfillment.

American psychiatrist, Dr. Aaron Beck, has described how such negative distortions in thinking can gradually lead people to the low opinion of themselves that is at the heart of depression.

How Emotions Influence Thinking

Psychological research has uncovered two ways in which emotional states influence thinking. Firstly, they color thinking by dictating the sorts of thought which enter consciousness. John Teasdale and his colleagues at Oxford University, England, have studied how mood affects the ability to remember. The influence is a clear one. In a low mood, people easily recall unhappy memories but find it harder to remember happy ones; a happy mood has the opposite effect. Obviously, this is one link in a vicious circle which can intensify an emotional state such as depression and make it very difficult for sufferers to break out by themselves. For example, one patient, as described by Aaron Beck, consistently told him about mainly gloomy events happening to her between their meetings. She was asked to keep a diary of daily events, and to her surprise discovered that most of the entries were ones she described as pleasing. Left to its own devices, her memory would selectively retrieve only the few negative ones, although in patients with major depressions memory and concentration are decreased for "neutral" objects as well.

The second way in which emotional states influence thinking emerges by considering the research into the effects of anxiety on reasoning and decision-making, and particularly the investigations carried out by American psychologist Charles Spielberger. Whether anxiety helps or hinders depends on the complexity of the task to be performed. Anxiety helps with tasks that are simple, but when Spielberger went on to study more complicated tasks the results were not so straightforward. In one study, he recorded the academic achievement (Grade-point average) of college stu-

months before she sought help for depression. First her marriage broke down and she started divorce proceedings; then she failed a driving test; later on she failed to secure a job for which she had been interviewed at a higher grade in the same company. Although the experience of a series of what are known as "stressful life events" has long been associated with depression, that this is not enough in itself to *cause* depression.

The crucial extra ingredient is amply displayed by this young woman. In every case, she could find no explanation outside of herself for what had happened, and she assumed an internal one: she was in her terms "incompetent, a bad wife, a poor driver, an incapable manager." She reached this conclusion despite the fact that her marriage broke up because of her husband's drinking, that she was entered for her driving test earlier than she thought wise, and that it was unlikely that someone as young as she was could have been offered the post for which she had been short-listed. The

Rigorous training and strict army discipline are designed to condition soldiers to cope with stress. Whether in a battle situation, or in a peace-keeping role, the smallest error of judgment could prove catastrophic.

In civilian life everyday stresses can build up and sometimes boil over. During the oil crisis of 1976, fights broke out in line-ups for gas — in a few cases shootings were even reported. People suffer most from

stress when there is nothing they can do to relieve the situation. The journey to and from work each day may be exhausting, but it is worse to be stuck in a tailback with nothing to do but wait.

dents for a single semester; their prior general level of anxiety had been assessed by questionnaire and their ability by an intelligence test. In the lowest-ability students, anxiety had no effect. In the very brightest ten per cent of the class, however, performance was better if they were also highly prone to anxiety. By contrast, students in the broad middle ranges of ability scored worse after the semester if they had also been highly anxious.

This research has implications for decision-makers. Where new solutions are needed to complex and important problems, anxiety in some decision-makers could cause an incorrect decision. Some situations, of course, combine extreme anxiety with demands for novel solutions to extremely complex and important problems.

Physical Illness and Emotions

Emotional states may influence physical health as well. It is possible that emotional reactions may trigger bodily processes that, unseen, increase a

Heavy bills to pay, trouble at work or at home, and even the daily diet of bad news in the press and on TV can lower the spirits of the most optimistic person. But people become suicidal only when facing almost

insurmountable personal problems, or when suffering deep, clinical depression. Statistics show that most who attempt suicide seek to draw attention to their plight, rather than actually wishing to die.

person's susceptibility to various disorders. Two examples are coronary heart diseases on the one hand, and cancers and infections on the other. The field of psychosomatics is devoted to the study of the relationship between "psyche," or mental processes, and "soma," or body.

The key to understanding this influence lies in the physiological changes that may underlie emotional reactions. An immediate physiological response to an emotional event results from the release of the hormone epinephrine by the adrenal glands. There are also other signals sent directly from the brain with similar effects. These are to increase the work done by the heart, to pump more blood around the tissues, and to contract blood vessels in the skin, thus diverting more blood to the muscles beneath. Breathing accelerates, providing more oxygen to be transported to the tissues via the rapidly circulating blood, and removing waste gases more efficiently. A fourth effect normally goes unnoticed; it is the release into the blood of fats normally stored in the body as a reserve for the production of energy.

This is no random set of responses but is carefully orchestrated. Fats, and oxygen to release their energy, are transported rapidly to the muscles of the body, preparing them to respond. During evolutionary history this reaction would have enabled humans — as it does other creatures — to respond to danger by the great muscular effort entailed in "fight or flight". Appropriately, one of the first physiologists to describe this process dubbed it the "emergency reaction."

The problem facing twentieth-century human beings in Western society is that few of the challenges they face can actually be dealt with by fight or flight. They have to address them, not by muscular, but by mental effort, which requires little energy. The circulating fats are not needed to release their energy and, by a process which still remains unclear, are redeposited in the body. Some are deposited in coronary arteries to form a plaque on the walls of the arteries, called atheroma. This can progress to detectable heart disease — angina or a heart attack — when an artery becomes so narrowed that the blood supply to the heart is insufficient.

Thus, it has been hypothesized that individuals

who are subjected to frequent emergency reactions are at elevated risk for heart disease. In some, for example, air traffic controllers, such risk is associated with extreme job stress. In others, it is associated with a particular constellation of personality characteristics. Two American cardiologists, Friedman and Rosenman, first described such people as "Type A" personalities, who are characterized by the trait of ambition, responsibility and hostility. The Type A individual has an excessive need to control events or other people, and to impose high standards or tight schedules which stretch coping resources to the limit. This is often the style of successful professional or managerial people, and their successes may carry the ultimate cost. Type A personalities were found to have up to five times other people's risk of heart disease, even after smoking and diet were taken into account. Research continues in an attempt to pinpoint the characteristics most associated with risk.

Everyone experiences depression at some stage of their lives, but when feelings of failure, inferiority and guilt become severe and prolonged, medical treatment is needed. The life of a depressive can be devastating, with victims retreating into themselves and refusing to talk or act in any way. Recent discoveries which have increased the efficacy of drug therapy, have successfully helped many depressives.

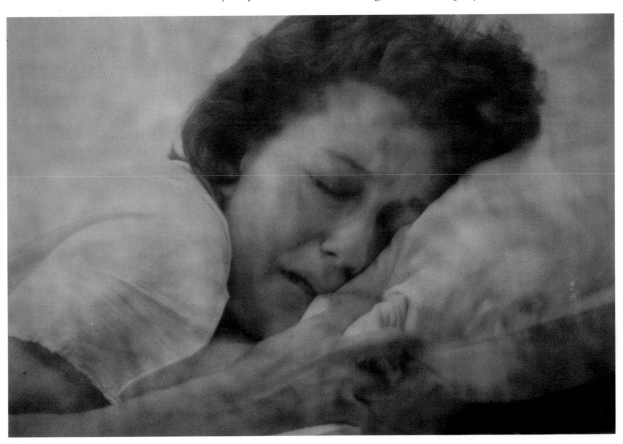

The stress research of Hans Seyle in Montreal has shown that the emergency reaction is only one part of the human emotional response to stress. Rather, he characterized this response as a three-stage "general adaptation syndrome," consisting of an alarm reaction, followed by a stage of resistance, and concluding with a stage of exhaustion.

Investigations have also begun to describe the physiological basis of stress response. One of the most important models, pioneered by the American researcher Vernon Riley, is that of the psychoendocrine immune axis, which links subjective emotion, hormone production and the immune system. It is believed that the production of adrenal cortical hormones rises under stress. According to the model, this increase, in turn, may weaken the action of the body's immune system. This system recognizes and neutralizes "foreign" substances, such as viruses and bacteria, thus protecting the body from illness. For this reason, recent investigators have sought to pinpoint a specific emotional response that may be linked to the onset or the progression of physical illness.

Thus far, the most promising candidate is the phenomenon of "learned helplessness," or distress combined with loss of control over the circumstances of distress, as described by the American psychologist Martin Seligman. In some studies, it has been suggested that the individuals in this state are more susceptible to infection and, even, the development of cancer. However, the research on stress and personality factors and illness is contradictory. Various workers have shown that psychological factors may, respectively, increase, decrease, or have no effect on the risk of illness or its progression.

Treatment for Emotional Problems

Psychological treatments for these physical disorders related to mental problems are in their

Most people have a dislike of spiders and try not to touch them or pick them up unless they have to. But for some people this fear is so intense as to become a phobia. Even the thought of spiders may fill them with dread *and provoke a frightening attack of anxiety. They may be unable to enter a strange house in case a spider is present. Anything can be the object of a phobia — heights, snakes, household dirt, cats, enclosed spaces* *and air travel are some of the commoner ones. Treatment often consists in a gradual exposure, under supervision, until patients come to terms with the object of their fear and are able to lead normal lives.*

infancy, although developing fast. They rely on finding ways of reducing people's negative emotional reactions, or of strengthening their capacities for positive, constructive thought and action. Similar techniques are already common in general psychiatry and clinical psychology and, for some anxious, phobic or depressed patients, may be helpful in addition to or as alternatives to using drugs. Although valuable aids to coping with short-term crises, in the long term many drugs alone are of less use in some cases. Two reasons for this have been discovered. The first is the remarkable adaptability of the nervous system, which quickly learns to compensate for the effects of some drugs (particularly antianxiety drugs), so that their potency diminishes. The second is that drugs may prevent the patient from learning to solve the problems which are causing the distress. It is precisely this sort of learning that is the goal of psychotherapy. On the other hand, there are cases in which drugs reduce the panic or anxiety to a less overwhelming level, so the patient can learn to cope with it. Then, as medication is gradually reduced, new learning strategies are incorporated.

Although a bewildering variety of psychotherapies is available, most divide fairly neatly into three major groups: behavioral, cognitive and psychodynamic psychotherapies. All the behavioral techniques start by having the patient *do* something. "Physiologically-oriented" techniques have the patient perform some exercise designed to relax the body and to reduce the arousal which underlies the emotional state. The number of these techniques grows each year. In one of the most common, progressive muscular relaxation, the patient is taught to relax each group of muscles in the body in turn. In autogenic training, the patient is taught to use vivid sensory descriptions or imagery to focus and intensify the relaxation process. In autohypnosis, the patient adds silent hypnotic suggestions of heaviness and relaxation. Although each procedure carries its own idiosyncrasies, the influential physician Dr. Herbert Benson has demonstrated that the relaxation response can be achieved by an appealingly simple technique. All that is needed is to learn to adopt a flexible, open, "let it happen" attitude, while focusing attention inward in quiet undistracting surroundings.

Electronic devices can now be used to convert some measure of arousal — heart rate, for example — into a signal which the patient can see or hear. Even small improvements, which could otherwise have gone unnoticed, can be made to start a light flashing faster or a tone sounding more

Research figures indicate a significant link between executive occupations and cardiovascular disease. Decision-making carries with it a burden of stress and anxiety. Fatty deposits may build up on artery walls, leading to high blood pressure and posssible cardiac arrest. Many company physicians recommend that staff practice relaxation techniques as a preventive step. These techniques consist of deep, regular breathing and the relaxation of body muscles or group of muscles in turn. Similar to eastern meditation practices (bottom), they are simply a way of telling the body that the emergency is over and it can return to normal.

loudly. This procedure, called biofeedback, is a valuable adjunct to relaxation training. Despite the short history in the West of such relaxation techniques, they are actually variations of the practice of meditation, used in oriental cultures for centuries.

Behavior therapy is another category of psychological treatment. It applies the principles of conditioned learning to the task of behavior change, either in the form of extinguishing symptomatic behavior or of increasing desirable behavior. An agoraphobic whose last five year's trips out alone have never taken her farther than the corner of the block must be gradually trained to travel farther before turning for home. An ''obsessional'' man who feels unbearably anxious and unclean when he has touched one of a variety of innocent household objects must be gradually trained to touch one of these items, without going on to carry out the washing ritual.

The most common technique is ''successive approximation''; the patient takes small steps at a time. The agoraphobic would be encouraged to travel along to the next corner for a few days until this causes little distress, then to the stores past the next block, and so on. The obsessional would be told to begin by touching an object which leaves him feeling only a little ''dirty''; when he can cope with this he would touch something a bit ''dirtier.''

One fact is clear about such techniques; they work powerfully on most people who want help. The way in which they work is not so clear. One current view supposes that being confronted with the dreaded situation allows patients to ''reassess'' their own responses to it. They are forced to experience their extreme discomfort in the situation. However, when they come to realize that they come to no harm and, especially after staying in the situation for a short while, the discomfort begins to decline. With time, a new more benign assessment of their reaction takes the place of their earlier distressing one. As a result, that reaction itself becomes less likely to occur.

Other Types of Therapy

An alternative approach to phobias and panic attacks involves the use of the tricyclic antidepressants in lower than antidepressant doses. These medications were demonstrated by the American

119

Behavioral psychologists see neuroses not as illnesses, but as undesirable habits that the patient has learned. Therapy consists of getting patients to unlearn the response which causes them their distress. The strip below

shows how this may be achieved in the case of someone suffering from agoraphobia, the fear of open spaces. The patient is first taken out with a therapist who reassures and calms her. With each session, they travel

farther, until the patient is ready to go out alone. Often, rewards are given — the patient may be encouraged to buy herself new clothes, for example, if she succeeds in going as far as the next block.

Mrs Smith would not go outdoors

Her therapist helped her step outside

Soon she could walk farther

The big day: she is able to leave home by herself

Each day she can venture farther from home

psychiatrist Dr. Donald Klein and others to be at least as effective as behavior therapy in the treatment of panic attacks. It is suggested that both the behavioral and pharmacological treatments for panic attacks work by the final common pathway of enabling the patient, with then decreased symptoms, to tolerate extended exposure to the initially feared event. Animal models of panic attacks also suggest that enduring the stimulus until the fearful reaction subsides is the curative element.

The cognitive therapy of Aaron Beck, and the rational-emotive therapy of Albert Ellis, are both designed to systematically correct the self-defeating misconceptions patients have of themselves or of others. The patient's negative distortions in thinking are identified and "restructured" in more realistic, adaptive terms. In this way, the depressive patient described earlier could be led to see that she is ignoring obvious external reasons for her failures when she blames herself. She

might then be shown how she sets unrealistic standards by which to judge her failure — how could she expect to secure such a high-powered job aged only twenty-eight? The success of cognitive psychotherapy testifies to the power of thoughts to control emotions.

Long-term psychoanalysis still owes much to the way Freud treated his own patients. It uses the relationship between the therapist and the patient as the focus for examination of the patient's inner thoughts. The former gives away no personal information, so that the patient's behavior toward him or her can reflect the expectations built up over previous relationships; this is the process called "transference." The therapist can then use his or her own relationship with the patient as a source of clues about problems which date back to those earlier ones.

For example, a certain male patient never complains to his male therapist — even when kept

Used in Freudian-type psychoanalysis, inkblot tests help to reveal a patient's fantasies and fears. The analyst notes which part of the blot the patient concentrates on and which parts are ignored, as well as the nature of the images and similarities that the patient sees. This gives the analyst an insight into the patient's problem. Such tests were first devised in the 1930s, and are still in extensive use.

waiting an hour for an appointment for which he himself is paying handsomely. This might suggest that he has learned in the past always to repress feelings of anger — perhaps originally to his father, but now to all adult males. The job of the therapist is to make this link between past and present clear to the patient.

Short-term psychodynamic psychotherapy is generally aimed at solving one or two of the patient's specific problems. Psychoanalysis, on the other hand, is aimed at producing widespread personality change, by an intensive program of similar techniques over a long period of time. There is little evidence that it achieves this, perhaps because studies to test the hypothesis are difficult to design, even if many people feel that they have been helped by it. Although they may seem quite distinct, most psychotherapies aim at the same goal — the elimination of painful and/or self-defeating behavior. In other words, they try to give patients more freedom. The differences lie in the ways they attempt to do this.

The Future

The sorts of disorders which can be helped in these ways are neuroses, in which patients feel alien to their personalities. Their reactions may be perplexing, but the things they react to are real. A different term, psychotic, is reserved for patients who appear to be responding to stimuli which are not real. They may hallucinate, reporting sights, sounds or smells which nobody else detects, or be deluded, describing strange beliefs which seem bizarre to normal people.

Until recently, it was presumed that the minds of patients such as this were deranged in some way; they simply did not operate according to the rules which normal — or neurotic — people follow. Some findings suggest that this may be a hasty conclusion. A group of patients who had recovered from schizophrenia — a relatively common psychosis — described having experienced frightening sights at the start of their illness. For example, some found that people and objects they looked at seemed to change size even as they watched, and sometimes to loom horrifyingly large in front of them.

These experiences as enduring phenomena are

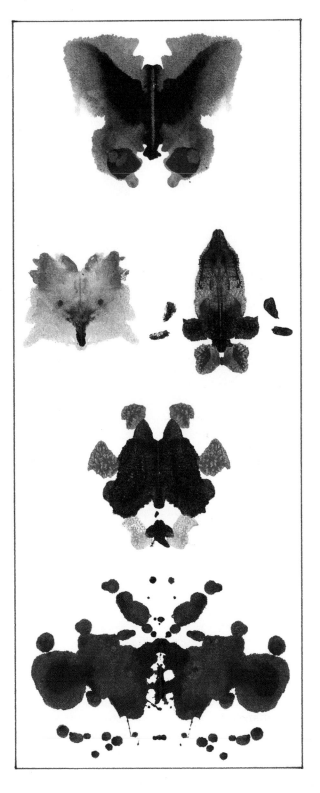

121

so far removed from those of most ordinary people that it may be hard for us to judge how we would react to them. With time, many of those patients adopted supernatural explanations for their experiences; they blamed evil spirits or extraterrestrial influences, or some patients began to think that they themselves had the power to change the properties of objects in the physical world around them. This showed that, at least in some cases, delusions may be the patient's way of "explaining" — having to find some reason for — bizarre and frightening sensations.

We can be fairly sure that these schizophrenic patients were not being influenced by supernatural forces, and that they were not really able, by the power of their minds, to influence the real world around them. The symptoms are improved or wholly treated by a class of medications which block the uptake of one neurotransmitter (dopamine), so it has been suggested that failure of regulation of this one chemical may be the original cause of the symptoms.

It is more difficult to be so confident in dismissing other claims for supernatural phenomena. For example, while many psychologists have often taken a dim view of religious belief, it continues to provide the only explanation for some phenomena many people are convinced exist. Even more controversial are the claims of some people to be able to change the shape or other properties of physical objects simply by the action of their own mind. Despite a great deal of research on such feats as Uri Geller's spoon-bending and similar phenomena, scientists remain unconvinced. They think that ultimately natural processes — sometimes devious ones — could have been at work. Scientists are, however, a generally cautious species. They rarely say categorically that a phenomenon does not exist. Instead they meet other people's faith with the reply "not proven."

Alfred Adler

An Individual Psychologist

In history it has often been the case that a person of short stature has been an effective — if not great — leader. To many psychologists this is quite understandable: the small person has compensated for a lack of stature by a dominating presence. It need not be size that is the determining factor in such a character, however; it could be some physical deformity, for example, some disability or some social deficiency — anything that might give rise to an "inferiority feeling" to which the individual reacts. This is the origin of the expression "inferiority complex," a concept first formulated by Alfred Adler, the Austrian psychologist and deviser of the psychological school called Individual Psychology.

Adler was born in February 1870 in Vienna. The son of a grain merchant, he grew up and was educated in that city. Gaining his medical doctorate at the University in 1895, he then spent two years in general medicine at Vienna's General Hospital before becoming more interested in therapies for mental illness. By 1902 he was closely associated with Sigmund Freud, and within a few years had become President of the Vienna Psychoanalytic Society. But like several others of Freud's circle, he became

gradually disenchanted with Freud's insistence on the primacy of sexuality in infancy as a cause of neurosis. In 1911 he made the decision to break away entirely, and to form his own movement.

For the next decade, Adler extended his ideas. His conviction that neurosis was specific to each individual and related to a perception of the individual's niche in society made him extremely socially conscious. One effect of this was his founding of the first child-guidance clinic in Vienna in 1921, counseling children, parents and teachers. From 1926 he took to making trips to the United States; he became visiting Professor at Columbia

University in 1927. And in 1932 — the year in which the Nazi party began to close down his child-guidance schools in Vienna — he emigrated permanently to become Professor of Psychiatry at Long Island College of Medicine in New York, at the age of sixty-two. Two years later, however, he died of a heart attack while on a lecture tour in Aberdeen, Scotland.

The basis of individual psychology was its relation solely to each individual patient. Adler saw neurosis as a maladroit attempt by a person at the kind of compensation described previously: it was over-compensation for the "inferiority feeling" specific to the patient that resulted in the neurosis. Treatment required the discovery of a unique life style that would restore the patient's confidence and reestablish equilibrium within the individual's society.

Despite Adler's exposition of his work in *Practice and Theory of Individual Psychology*, published in 1927, he did not formalize his methods or establish a corresponding means of analysis for psychiatric therapy. This, with the fact that much of his later writings were more general, has had the result that, since his death, his work has lost something of its initial impact.

Chapter 6

Modifying Behavior

Consider the following situation. A group of people were asked to carry out a very boring task, adding up long lists of numbers without a pocket calculator. After doing so, some of them were offered a dollar to go into a waiting room to tell another group of volunteers that the task was fun and interesting. Others were offered fifty dollars to do the same thing. Afterward all of them — those who got one dollar and those who got fifty — were asked for their real opinion of the task they took part in. Contrary to what most people might anticipate, it was the one-dollar group who said they enjoyed it most.

Why should this be so? As a result of the procedure they went through, the one-dollar group may have said to themselves: "I have just done two boring tasks and then told someone that they were fun and interesting, for which I have been paid only one dollar. It cannot be the money I told that lie for, because such a small amount was involved. The only explanation for my deceiving another person must be that the task was really not so boring at all. So I was not telling a lie." The fifty-dollar group have no such problems. They just lied (and it was not really a very serious lie) because they were paid handsomely to do so.

Thus if a man (or woman) is bribed to act contrary to his beliefs and if the amount is small, he will probably say to himself: "I have been bought for a pathetic, paltry sum." To stop feeling that he is a "cheap bribe," he will tend to come to believe that he acted the way he did, not because of a paltry sum but because he really believed in what he did. On the other hand, if he has been bought for a large sum, he will tend to explain his conduct by saying to himself: "No one could resist such a great sum — everyone else would do the same," and therefore he will not find it necessary to counter the threat to his self-image of a moral, respectable person by changing his attitudes. This phenomenon, of ascribing greater value to deeds that have required personal sacrifice, is a well-

The head of Michelangelo's David *forms an appropriate frame for a world pulsating with energy. Chipping away at the Newtonian model of the universe as a Great Machine, researchers are beginning to express their findings in terms of a Great Mind whose constructs are less a result of inflexible laws as of human perception and interaction with them.*

Young minds are easily manipulated, and in the 1930s Nazi propaganda often exploited the innocence of children in a drive toward achieving what was defined by the Nazi leaders as a "pure" race.

known concept in social psychology, described by the American psychologist Leon Festinger.

A Foot in the Door

How do you get people to agree to their homes being searched by strangers? A group of researchers posing as members of a consumer group telephoned several hundred homemakers. They were asked if they would agree to allow a team of people to thoroughly interview them about various domestic products and to allow the team to have complete freedom in searching the whole house including closets, cabinets and drawers.

In one group of home owners, this excessive request was made immediately, during a single phone call. Another group, were called twice. On the first telephone call, they were presented with a simple, small request: would they agree to answer a few simple questions about the types of toilet soap that they used? A few days later they were phoned by the same person asking them to agree to the visit of the team. Only 22.2 per cent of the homeowners called once agreed, whereas 52.8 per

cent of those who were called twice consented.

When people comply with an initial small request they often experience small but important changes in the way they see themselves. For instance, they may come to view themselves as kind or concerned with helping others. As a result of these changes, they may be more likely to agree to a second, larger request. Hence the importance of the foot-in-the-door principle — a small request followed by a large request.

But what about its opposite: a large request first, followed by a second smaller request? Imagine you were stopped in the street and asked if you would act as a non-paid counselor for three hours a week for a two-year period. Few people would agree, but then if the requestor had a fall-back proposal that you volunteered to take some handicapped children to the zoo for two hours, would you agree? The answer is probably yes — you would be much more likely to agree.

One explanation for this strategy is that it involves pressure toward reciprocal concessions. When an individual who starts out with a very

126

large request (such as a demand for a raise) backs down to a much smaller one, the person receiving these requests may be compelled to make a corresponding concession. This seems reasonable because the requestor has agreed to meet them halfway, so the least one can do is reciprocate. Hence the usefulness of the door-in-the-face principle — a large request then a small one.

But how can starting with a small request and shifting to a larger one, and starting with a large one and then backing down both result in increased compliance? Simply because they are based on different principles, so that the two techniques can both be effective, but under somewhat different conditions. For the door-in-the-face approach to succeed, it must involve two requests by the same person. If someone has refused a large request from one person, there is no reason why he or she should experience pressure to make a concession to a different person. By contrast, the foot-in-the-door technique works quite well even when different persons make the first and second requests. If an individual has experienced shifts in self-perception as a result of agreeing to an initial small request, these changes may well carry over to a new situation — one in which a larger request is presented by another person. Both these techniques are used, particularly by salesmen and saleswomen, to influence behavior.

Shocked to Death

Would you follow an order to apply potentially lethal shocks to a totally innocent victim? When he was tried for killing a hundred innocent and defenceless Vietnamese villagers, Lieutenant Calley argued that he was merely following orders. Those were times of war and soldiers are under great pressure and stress.

But what would happen in a quiet part of New Haven, Connecticut? The American psychologist Stanley Milgram recruited forty ordinary American men of various ages and occupations to take part in an experiment for a fee. They were told that the purpose of the study was to determine the effects of punishment on learning. They drew lots for the role of teacher and learner but, unknown to them, the draw was rigged so that they were always teachers and an accomplice of the psychologist —

an actor — was always the learner. The psychologist was present throughout the experiment.

The "learner" was strapped to a chair and electrodes attached to his wrist. The volunteer "teacher" read a series of word pairs (blue box, wild duck) to the "learner," and then read the first word of the pair along with four other words. The learner's job was to indicate which of the four words was correct by pressing a switch that lit a lamp in the teacher's room.

The teacher was told to administer a shock to the learner each time he gave a wrong response, using a shock generator with thirty separate switches which increased by 15-volt increments from 15 to 450 volts. These were labeled from "Slight Shock" at the low end to "Danger: Severe Shock" and finally "XXX" at the top end. This equipment was fake and the learner (the actor) never actually received a shock, but pretended that he did.

After each wrong answer (of which the learner made many), the psychologist instructed the teacher to move one level higher on the shock generator. When the teacher reached 300 volts, the learner began to pound on the wall between the two rooms and, from then on, no longer made any answer to the questions posed by the subject. At this point, teachers usually turned to the psychologist for guidance. In a firm and rather stern voice, the psychologist replied that no answer was to be treated as wrong and the subject was to be shocked according to the proper schedule.

What the psychologist was interested in was how many subjects would continue to administer shocks to the end of the series, following his orders. Of the forty volunteers, twenty-six (sixty-five per cent) continued to the end of the shock series, and not a single person stopped before administering 300 volts — the point at which the learner began pounding the wall. Five refused to obey at that point. A total of fourteen subjects refused at some point. Milgram concluded that obedience to commands is a strong force in our society, because nearly two-thirds of his volunteers obeyed his instructions even though they were strongly led to believe that they were hurting another human being.

Many other studies of obedience to authority followed this one, and although they revealed many different factors to be important in predicting obedience, study after study found substantially the same result: people often obey orders which overrule personal scruples and persuade a person to perform acts that he or she would otherwise find unacceptable.

The aim of psychology, as in any other social or behavioral science, is to understand the mind and behavior. A full understanding of the mind would allow for accurate predictions of behavior — and ultimately the opportunity to influence behavior. Of course, being able to control behavior means that psychological knowledge could be used for good as well as for evil. Being able to detect when people are not telling the truth by using a lie detector or some other device may be one method used by the police or by lawyers in an attempt to detect criminals, but it may also be used by criminals to gain vital information from people whom they have kidnapped.

There are therefore many possible advantages and disadvantages of new knowledge. Consider, for example, the present understanding of inter-personal behavior. From what psychologists and psychiatrists know about verbal and nonverbal communication, they can teach people to be better communicators by using social skills training. This may help people in their private and professional lives. The acquisition of social skills may considerably help people train to become better interviewers, salesmen, therapists, counselors, teachers, public speakers, supervisors and managers.

But giving people new knowledge of interpersonal behavior may have various undesirable consequences. Firstly, their behavior may become more artificial and insecure — more like acting than being themselves. Secondly, they may become self-conscious, awkward and unspontaneous during the learning of the skills. Thirdly, people may be manipulated by practitioners of the new skills — for instance, they may be persuaded to buy things they neither want nor can afford; or they may put undue trust in teachers or therapists.

Manipulating Sales: Consumer Behavior

We are bombarded with hundreds of advertisements every day — on the radio and television; in newspapers and magazines; on billboards and in stores. What determines whether we even attend to them, let alone follow their advice?

Consumer psychologists are concerned with the effectiveness of communication between the producers and consumers of goods. Through large surveys, as well as in-depth marketing interviews and tests, psychologists hope to uncover attitudes and feelings toward products as well as unconscious motives for purchasing or not purchasing. They also try to measure what people actually do. Numerous methods include analysis of sales records; actual observations of purchases (by whom, when and where purchases are made); people's ability to identify and distinguish between various brands; and analysis of coupon returns.

An understanding of the purchasing process requires knowledge of three things. It requires knowledge of the consumers — their personality, socioeconomic class, age, sex, ethnic-group membership, buying habits and brand loyalty. Each of these variables affects why, where, with whom and with how much they shop for goods. Then there is the product — its package, which may

reflect convenience, security, status, dependability or beauty, its image and its price. Finally there is the advertising message — the medium it is delivered in, the consumer need it is targeting, whether it is positive (pleasant consequences of product purchase) or negative (unpleasant consequences of product non-purchase).

The research in this area is voluminous. But there are three particularly interesting and relevant areas for the psychologist: the nature of persuasive messages; the most effective medium for advertising; and the effects of subliminal perception.

Persuasive advertising messages are written, spoken, televised and filmed to present potential purchasers with facts and arguments to attempt to alter (or sometimes maintain) their attitudes to buy. Perhaps the most important aspect of the message is credibility, trustworthiness or believability. A consumer's perception of credibility is based upon the advertiser or communicator's apparent expertise — knowledge, experience — and the advertiser's apparent motives, that is, what they have to lose or to gain.

Communicators who are high in expertise and positive motives are viewed as credible. They are, as a result, quite successful at persuasion. The reverse is also true — communicators with little apparent expertise and questionable (selfish) motives have low credibility and are not persuasive. Thus if a top sportsman recommends a sporting product and, because of his wealth, appears to be promoting the product out of conviction rather than for profit, people are more likely to buy.

Of course, the clarity, forcefulness or memorableness of the advertisement is important. It also seems that advertisements that present a balanced argued view which attempts to demolish the opposition are more effective in changing attitudes than simple one-sided arguments. What about stimulating strong emotions like anger, anxiety or fear

The Secret by FRANK HANLEY

THE Only SECRET IS THE ONE NEVER TOLD!

Advertising that aims to warn against a potential hazard, such as betraying national secrets, must be carefully pitched: too much emotional impact is less likely, rather than more likely, to alter behavior.

among viewers or readers? It appears that such fear-inducing advertisements (for example, against germs) are most successful in altering attitudes if, and only if, they generate moderate levels of emotional arousal. If too weak, they have little impact; if too strong, they are often ignored. The persons who see or hear them must believe that the dangers cited are real, and that the recommendations for avoiding the dangers (by using the product) will be effective.

Is it better to advertise on the television, on the radio, in newspapers and magazines, or on billboards? Factors such as cost and audience determine this decision just as much as effectiveness. Television not only costs more than radio (to produce and broadcast) but it reaches a different audience. The sex, age, socioeconomic status and so on of audiences varies enormously, and wise advertisers choose their medium carefully.

A number of psychological studies have been undertaken to look at such factors as a person's memory for the same material presented in newspapers and magazines (print), on radio (audio) and on television (audio-visual). Contrary to many people's beliefs, research seems to show that an audience tends to remember least information received through the television and most through the print medium. This corresponds with evidence to the effect that learning from television news is less efficient than learning from newsprint. There

are various explanations for this. Partly it has to do with the way each medium is used by the public, but partly also it is linked with inherent characteristics of audio-visual and written materials and the way individuals cognitively process them.

The fact that more learning seems to occur from newspapers than from the broadcast media of radio or television may indicate something about the inherent capacities of these different media to convey knowledge to their respective consumers. One study, for example, reported that 57 per cent of a survey sample were able to recall, in fairly complete detail, news stories they had read about in the newspapers during the previous twenty-four hours, whereas only about 45 per cent could recall as much detail of stories seen on television.

Differential Recall

One explanation for such different levels of information recall may lie with the way news is presented in newspapers compared with on the broadcast media. Newspapers can cover stories in much more detail than radio or television news bulletins. News broadcasts have restricted airtime. The narrative of a standard half-hour television bulletin, for instance, carries less content than the front page of a serious broadsheet newspaper.

Another reason for different recall from print and broadcast media may be that newspaper reading is self-paced, whereas on radio and television the rate at which the news is presented is determined by the program-maker. The listener or viewer has no opportunity, once an item has been presented, to go back over it again and check details. Despite this, experimental studies in which the same materials have been presented audio-visually, in audio only, or in print, and where exposure time is equalized across viewers, listeners or readers, have found different levels of recall of the same stories from different modalities. Of course remembering an advertisement is different from buying a product. But research does seem to show that to teach people something, the best medium remains the printed page.

Does information through hidden messages and subliminal advertising work? The idea behind subliminal perception is that stimuli (pictures, sounds, and so on) which are too weak or too briefly

Research suggests that information presented on the printed page is more likely to be retained than that broadcast on television or radio. Consumer psychologists are employed by advertisers — who spend more on print than any other form of advertising — to obtain maximum benefit. Typically, the sex, age and socioeconomic status of a readership are assessed to determine which publication to use.

presented to enter conscious experience may, nevertheless, be subconsciously processed. That is, although people may not be aware of the stimulus (a split-second picture of a snake, for example), it may nevertheless be possible to detect a response to it. Furthermore, their verbal responses are qualitatively quite different from those elicited by the same stimulus presented above the awareness threshold. Subliminal stimulation has been shown to affect dreams, memory, perception, verbal behavior and emotional responses.

In the late 1950s, people became aware of the possible commercial and political gains through subliminal stimulation. They wondered whether a subliminal advertisement ("Eat more popcorn") or political slogan ("Vote Republican") could make someone, or at least encourage someone, to do something which he or she might otherwise refrain from doing. Some experimental evidence seems to suggest that this is a possibility, but there

are three good reasons to suppose that it is rarely if ever effective.

Firstly, there are enormous individual differences in the thresholds of awareness. It is impossible to find an intensity or duration value for the "subliminal" advertisement without missing out on some people altogether or reaching some at the level of consciousness. Age, and position relative to the screen, would probably alone be sufficient to account for the advertisement being below the physiological threshold for a sizable proportion of the audience.

Secondly, for subliminal perception to work, the viewer needs to be in a relaxed, passive state. Because a person cannot attend to a stimulus of which he or she is unaware, any other ongoing supraliminal stimulation which attracts attention will almost certainly swamp the effect of a simultaneously presented subliminal advertisement. Thus if a sub- and supraliminal stimulus are pre-

Almost one in ten people will suffer from a mental illness at some time. Such illnesses can be divided into four broad categories. Neuroses are characterized by depression, multiple personality, obsessions and phobias.

Brain damage is one cause of the more serious symptoms of psychosis, including delusions of grandeur or persecution, the withdrawal from reality of schizophrenia and the highs and lows of manic depression.

Stressful living can take its toll in psychosomatic complaints of rashes, raised blood pressure, ulcers and asthma. Personality disorders commonly are as much a threat to society as to the individual.

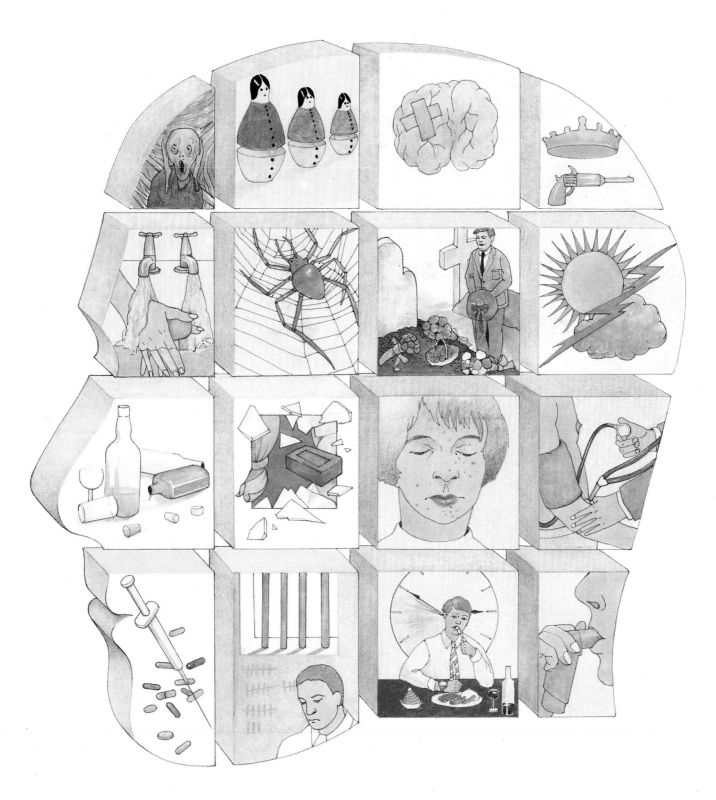

With a lack of compassion typical of its time, an eighteenth-century engraving depicts mentally-disturbed inmates at Bethlehem Royal Hospital, one of the first asylums for the insane in England.

Like something out of Disneyland, the nineteenth-century castle of Neuschwanstein (right) was a product of the fantastical imagination of Ludwig II — an imagination that soon degenerated into madness.

sented together, the latter often swamps the former. It is very easy to prevent a weak stimulus from having an effect by swamping it.

Thirdly, whereas a subliminal advertisement may affect verbal behavior (stated preferences), it is unlikely to have any major effect on other overt acts of choice. For instance, in one study subjects were shown the word "Beef" for one-twohundredth of a second, every seven seconds, during the course of watching a supraliminal film. Following this they rated themselves for hunger and were then encouraged to choose one from an assortment of different sandwiches. The results showed that, whereas the subliminal stimulus word 'Beef'' had a significant effect upon subsequent hunger-ratings, it did not affect subsequent choice behavior. Beef sandwiches were not chosen significantly more often than others. Evidently, feelings of hunger were increased, but without any discernible effect upon existing food preferences.

So, attractive though the techniques may seem to advertisers, it would appear that nobody need fear the power of these hidden persuaders.

Healing the Ill Mind

Mental illness may be the worst epidemic of all time. One in every ten people in the United States will, at some time, receive treatment for mental illness. Many others self-medicate with alcohol, nicotine, drugs or tranquilizers. Some consult astrologers, their family doctor, herbalists or a local priest, while many others go to psychologists or psychiatrists. They are all seeking relief from distress — a healing of the mind.

For many years the description, categorization, and therefore diagnosis of mental disorders was difficult because different experts used different criteria and terminology. For example, terms such as "psychoneurosis," introduced by Freud and later shortened to "neurosis," were given various

interpretations. Then in the United States the American Psychiatric Association standardized the nomenclature in its definitive publication *Diagnostic and Statistical Manual of Mental Disorders*. The third edition, usually referred to as *DSM–III*, recognizes up to seventeen major categories of mental disorders, many with various subcategories. The chief ones, with brief descriptions, are described in the following paragraphs.

Childhood Disorders

DSM–III lists several subcategories under the heading "Disorders Usually First Evident in Infancy, Childhood or Adolescence." Mental retardation is defined in terms of subaverage intellectual ability (an IQ of seventy or less) with impairment of adaptive behavior and with onset before the age of eighteen years. Behavior illnesses are divided into attention deficit disorder, with or without hyperactivity, and conduct disorder, which is subdivided according to the degree of socialization and aggressiveness. Attention deficit disorder is characterized by inattention and impulsivity inappropriate to the child's stage of development. A persistent, repetitive pattern of conduct which

violates social norms appropriate to the child's age is an essential feature of conduct disorder.

Two of the subclasses of anxiety disorders of childhood and adolescence focus on specific situations: separation anxiety disorder and avoidance anxiety disorder. The first manifests itself as an unwillingness to take trips independently away from the home — even to attend school — whereas in the second there is a persistent avoidance of contact with strangers but a clinging attitude to family members. The third subclass, over-anxious disorder, involves nonspecific worrying and fearful behavior. Timidity and difficulty in getting to sleep are often symptomatic of these anxiety states.

Several other disorders in this age range include reactive attachment disorder, manifest in infants who have lacked adequate care resulting in a failure to thrive physically and develop emotionally, and schizoid disorder of childhood or adolesence, in which normal social relationships are lacking but the child is apparently not distressed by the resulting isolation — he or she is a "loner," except possibly in a relationship with a similarly isolated child. In elective mutism, the child persist-

ently refuses to talk at school and in social situations (although having the ability to understand spoken language and to speak).

A child suffering from oppositional disorder, aged between three and eighteen years, is persistently disobedient and negativistic, often with temper tantrums or stubbornness, although still recognizing the basic rights of others.

The final subclass in this overall category is identity disorder, in which self-doubt is coupled with mild anxiety and depression. Uncertainty about such issues as moral values, group loyalties and long-term goals leads to severe distress.

Eating disorders range from anorexia nervosa, in which a fear of becoming obese does not diminish as self-imposed starvation brings about an alarming loss in weight, to bulimia, in which there are recurrent binges of overeating, often punctuated by episodes of dieting or self-induced vomiting. Children suffering from the rare disorder of pica eat non-food substances, such as paint, plaster, leaves or even pebbles. The chief feature of the even rarer rumination disorder of infancy is regurgitation of food (without nausea or gastrointestinal disorder) for at least a month, consequently with no gain in weight or perhaps a loss in weight.

An abnormality of gross motor muscle control is the essential characteristic of stereotyped movement disorders in children. Most involve the rapid involuntary movement of muscles that produces tics, and most are statistically more common in boys than in girls. Other childhood mental disorders — some persisting through adulthood — with physical manifestations include stuttering, functional enuresis (bed-wetting) and functional encopresis (involuntary and inappropriate defecation), none of which is caused by a purely physical disorder. Again most sufferers are boys.

Sleepwalking disorder involves repeated episodes, lasting from several minutes to half an hour, which cannot be recalled on waking, and which take place during non-REM sleep (30 to 200 minutes after the onset of sleep). As with sleep terror disorder, in which the child repeatedly wakes with a panicky scream, it is an essential feature of the diagnosis that the episodes take place during non-REM sleep — that is, not during the normal stages of dreaming. Again the child can

seldom remember the experience the next day.

Developmental disorders are of two types. Distortions in the development of psychological functions pertaining to language and social skills — such as attention, and perception and motor movement — characterize pervasive developmental disorders. They include infantile autism, in which the child is incapable of responding to others but perhaps makes bizarre responses to inanimate objects. Specific developmental disorders include the reading difficulties commonly refered to as dyslexia or "word blindness" and similar arithmetic and language disorders. In developmental articulation disorder, the later-acquired speech sounds (such as "r," "sh," "th" and "ch") fail to develop, giving rise to a lisp or the impression of "baby talk."

Organic Mental Disorders

This major category includes transient or permanent dysfunctions of the brain that give rise to psychological or behavioral disorders — that is, the cause is known (or presumed). One group includes dementias resulting from neurological diseases and "substance-induced" disorders, such

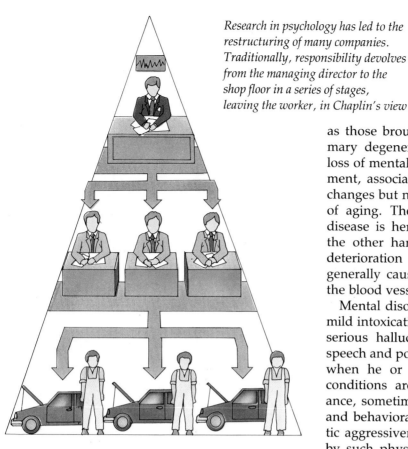

Research in psychology has led to the restructuring of many companies. Traditionally, responsibility devolves from the managing director to the shop floor in a series of stages, leaving the worker, in Chaplin's view (right), as a mere "cog in the machinery." Increasingly, productivity is seen to be linked to a less rigid structure, with workers involved in a wider range of tasks and contributing to company policy.

as those brought about by alcohol or drugs. Primary degenerative dementia involves a gradual loss of mental abilities, such as memory and judgment, associated with personality and behavioral changes but not attributable to the normal process of aging. The type known also as Alzheimer's disease is hereditary. Multi-infarct dementia, on the other hand, is characterized by a "patchy" deterioration in intellectual functioning, and is generally caused by vascular disease that affects the blood vessels of the brain.

Mental disorders caused by alcohol range from mild intoxication, through withdrawal delirium to serious hallucinosis and dementia. The slurred speech and poor coordination of a drunk get better when he or she sobers up. The more serious conditions are associated with alcohol dependance, sometimes worsened by vitamin deficiency, and behavioral changes — such as uncharacteristic aggressiveness — which may be accompanied by such physical symptoms as nausea and high blood pressure.

Substance-induced organic mental disorders are defined in terms of the drugs concerned: barbiturates, opioids, cocaine, amphetamines, phencyclidine (PCP), hallucinogens (specifically LSD-type and mescaline-type), cannabis, tobacco (withdrawal), caffeine, and others. It should be remembered that this category concerns drug-induced disorders for which there is an organic (that is, brain-damaging) cause, and is different from substance use disorders (described later).

The other major group of organic mental disorders are refered to as organic brain syndromes, in which there is a collection of behavioral or psychological symptoms with no obvious cause. They include delirium, involving blurring of consciousness accompanied by such symptoms as illusions, hallucinations, incoherent speech or insomnia; dementia; amnesia (impairment of both short-term and long-term memory); organic delusional syndrome, with persistent delusions; organic affective syndrome involving manic or depressive mood disturbances; organic personality syndrome, a marked personality or behavioral change associated with emotional outbursts, social or sexual indiscretions, apathy or paranoid inclinations; and intoxication and withdrawal, ranging

from the mild impairment caused by tobacco to the severe results of taking alcohol or opioids.

Substance Use Disorders

This category is reserved for abnormal behavior accompanying the regular use of drugs and other substances, as opposed to the substance-induced group of organic mental disorders caused by direct effects on the central nervous system. Within the category, distinction is made between abuse and dependence. The former involves a pattern of pathological use affecting functioning in a social or work situation with a disturbance lasting at least a month. Dependance involves both tolerance, in which the individual requires a progressively larger "dose" of the substance to achieve the desired effect, and also withdrawal, the collection of symptoms that follows when the individual stops (or reduces) the intake of the substance. The substances are classified in the same way as those in substance-induced organic mental disorders.

Schizophrenic Disorders

Schizophrenia is one of the most difficult mental disorders to define. According to *DSM–III,* the disorder begins before the age of forty-five and lasts for at least six months. There is an observable deterioration from previous levels of functioning socially, at work or at home. Multiple psychological processes, such as thinking, perception and psychomotor behavior, are disturbed.

Disturbance in the content of thought may lead to delusions as bizarre as "thought broadcasting" or a belief in external control of thoughts and deeds. Hallucinations result from disturbances in perception, particularly the auditory hallucination of "hearing voices." Impaired psychomotor behavior may lead to a reduction in movement from the extreme of catatonic rigidity, in which the individual remains immobile, to the other of catatonic excitement and posturing. Schizophrenia is also typified by the presence of psychotic features during its active phase.

Paranoid Disorders

Persistent delusions of persecution are the chief features of paranoid disorders, which are sometimes difficult to differentiate from other mental states, such as schizophrenia. Usually a single theme (or connected set of themes) runs through the delusions, which vary from a belief of being spied upon or conspired against to being drugged or poisoned. In some patients, the key feature of the disorder is delusional jealousy, in which the

patient entertains the mistaken belief that his or her partner is being unfaithful.

Affective Disorders

Also known as mood disorders, this category includes mental disorders that involve full or partial manic depressive syndrome accompanying a prolonged emotional disturbance that affects psychic life. The key feature is usually elation or depression.

An individual with a major affective disorder has a manic episode or a major depressive one. In mania the predominant mood is usually elation or irritability, manifest in such symptoms as hyperactivity, enlarged self-esteem and flights of fancy. It may be that only people who know the individual well recognize the behavior as excessive; to others it may appear merely as infectious euphoria. But if the individual is thwarted, irritability may come to the fore. A marked decrease in the need for sleep is another typical characteristic.

A major depressive episode involves dysphoria — generally depression — or a lack of pleasure in most normal activities. Accompanying symptoms may include disturbance in sleep or appetite, leading to weight change, feelings of guilt or worthlessness, sometimes leading to thoughts of death or suicide. These symptoms are often recognized sooner by family or friends than by the individual, who may be agitated or exhibit retarded psychomotor activity characterized by slow speech and slow body movements. In either case, the individual may complain of fatigue.

Other affective disorders include cyclothymic disorder, in which a mood disturbance lasting for at least two years involves many periods of mania or depression, often interspersed with times of normal mood, and dysthymic disorder. Also known as depressive neurosis, dysthymic disorder has as its chief feature a long-lasting mood disturbance involving depression or lack of interest in most normal activities. Both differ from major affective disorders only in severity and duration.

Anxiety Disorders

Affecting an estimated two to four per cent of the population at some time in their lives, anxiety disorders include various phobias and anxiety states. The key feature of a phobic disorder (or neurosis) is an irrational fear of some object or

140

situation, which is nevertheless recognized by the individual to be excessive or unreasonable. The avoidance behavior is sufficient to cause deep distress or to interfere with normal living (not merely, for example, as in the common dislike of snakes or spiders).

Agoraphobia is the most severe phobic disorder. The individuals fear being alone or in public places from which they cannot easily escape (such as in elevators, public transport or in a busy crowded street). They often refuse to go out unless accompanied by a friend or relative. Panic attacks may also be a feature.

In social phobia the fear is of scrutiny by others, in case of humiliation or embarrassment; in ordinary terms, it is extreme shyness. The individual recognizes the behavior as unreasonable, which in turn leads to more distress.

Anxiety states include panic disorder, generalized anxiety, and various forms of obsessive or compulsive behavior. Recurrent attacks of panic characterize panic disorder, which may occur unpredictably or in certain situations (such as catching an airplane), which the individual comes to anticipate. Shortness of breath, sweating, trembling and various other "fear" symptoms accompany the attacks.

Persistent general anxiety for at least a month characterizes generalized anxiety disorder, without specific symptoms of other anxiety states. There may be motor tension, with trembling or twitching; autonomic hyperactivity, expressed in such ways as sweating, dizziness and upset stomach; apprehensive expectation, in which the individual worries that something bad is about to happen; and hyperattentiveness, involving edginess and impatience, often with sleep problems.

Recurrent obsessions or compulsions dominate obsessive compulsive disorder (or neurosis). Obsessions are persistent ideas or images that invade the consciousness as senseless thoughts, which the individual tries to suppress or ignore. Compulsions involve purposeful behavior carried out repetitively according to some sort of ritual in a mistaken attempt to influence some future situation. Again the individual is usually aware of the senselessness of the behavior, but just "cannot help himself." Common obsessions include repeti-

Erik Erikson

The Individual and Identity

The Sioux nation of Pine Ridge Reservation in 1938 must have been surprised to find themselves playing host to a contemporarily well known psychoanalytical clinician from Harvard Medical School, as he studied their culture and especially their ideas on bringing up children. The Yurok Indians of northern California were probably equally astonished to perform the same office the following year. Yet it was all part of Erik Homburger Erikson's research that led to a profound series of essays, later published as a textbook: *Childhood and Society*.

Erikson was born in Frankfurt am Main, West Germany, in June 1902. Brought up by his Danish mother and German stepfather, he left school to study art in Munich. After spending some time in Florence, he eventually arrived in Vienna in 1927 and quickly found himself teaching in a small day school run by Sigmund Freud's daughter Anna. Influenced there by psychoanalysis — he met Freud and underwent analysis himself with Anna — and by new theories of education (he studied the methods propagated by Maria Montessori), Erikson was fascinated and learned rapidly. He was particularly interested in theoretical psychoanalysis, in

the furtherance of which he himself began to interview children as patients. His first paper was published in 1930, after which he was elected a member of the Vienna Psychoanalytic Society. His work had gained him such authority in the field that, on emigrating with his Canadian wife to the United States in 1933, he was able to set up a psychoanalytical practice in Boston, although he had no formal university qualifications.

In a very short time, Erikson was teaching in the faculty at Harvard Medical School. He was in contact with such eminent personages as Kurt Lewin and Margaret Mead, and carrying out important research into the creative capacity of the

ego (the human consciousness). In 1936 he transferred to the Institute of Human Relations at Yale, and it was from there that his two studies of Native American culture were undertaken. Erikson then became Professor of Psychology at the University of California at Berkeley until 1950 when, confronted by a demand to sign an oath of loyalty dissociating himself from Communist organizations, he refused on principle and took once more to work as a clinician. By 1960, however, he was Professor of Human Development and lecturer in psychiatry at Harvard; he officially retired in 1970.

Childhood and Society, Erikson's first and most famous book (edited by his wife), was in the direct tradition of Freud, and extended it to explain in greater detail the relationship between individual development and cultural environment; special attention was paid to the function of play. Incorporating many of Erikson's profound insights, the work concentrated on the concept of identity, commenting on different types of societies and individuals.

Other publications included analytical considerations on the life and activities of Martin Luther, Adolf Hitler and Mahatma Gandhi.

tive thoughts of violence, contamination (for example, of catching a disease by touching door handles) or doubt. Hand-washing and repetitive touching are common compulsions.

Post-traumatic stress disorder involves symptoms that develop after a psychologically traumatic event that is not experienced by most people. That is, common life crises such as divorce, serious illness or bereavement do not produce such symptoms, which are more likely to be triggered by traumas such as rape, military combat, or a disastrous fire or plane crash. The individual may reexperience the event (mentally), develop numbed responses to the environment, or exhibit various symptoms such as hyperalertness, nightmares and memory impairment.

Somatoform Disorders

Disorders formerly described as hysteria are typical of somatoform disorders, in which there are

physical symptoms but no organic disorder to account for them. In somatization disorder there are various somatic complaints over a period of several years, usually before the age of thirty; medical advice has been sought but no physical causes found. The individual may describe the symptoms in an exaggerated or dramatic way, and include such wide-ranging "disorders" as blindness, paralysis, pain and dizziness.

Conversion disorder, or hysterical neurosis, is subtly different. An alteration in physical functioning (which suggests but is not caused by a physical disorder) disguises some psychological need or conflict. The most common "symptoms" are neurological (blindness, paralysis, and so on), but also include vomiting (representing revulsion) and false pregnancy. The symptom may provide an excuse for the individual to avoid some undesirable activity or to solicit support from others.

In psychogenic pain disorder the predominant

symptom is pain (without a diagnosable physical cause), whereas in hypochondriasis the individual has an irrational belief that he or she is suffering from a serious disorder, and misinterprets physical signs as abnormal even when given medical reassurance that there is nothing organically wrong.

Dissociative Disorders

The chief feature of dissociative disorders is a sudden, but temporary, change in consciousness, identity or motor behavior. Typically, memory is affected, or the individual adopts a new identity, or becomes a wanderer. In psychogenic amnesia there is an inability to recall significant personal information. It may be localized, relating to events from a particular period of time (often immediately following a traumatic event); selective, in which only some events cannot be recalled; generalized, involving memory loss extending back to infancy; or continuous, lasting up to the present.

An individual with psychogenic fugue makes a sudden trip away from home and adopts a new identity, with no recollection of the previous one. The event cannot subsequently be remembered, even after recovery. With multiple personality, however, two or more different personalities exist within the same individual, with one personality dominating at any particular time and determining behavior. In depersonalization disorder, the perception of self suddenly changes.

Psychosexual Disorders

There are four main groups of psychosexual disorders. Those involving gender identity include transsexualism, in which the individual has a persistent desire to change sex and may request sex-change therapy to achieve this desire. Paraphilias, or sexual deviations, are disorders involving bizarre imagery or acts to achieve sexual arousal, and include such extremes as bondage, sadism and masochism. Fetishism (the use of nonliving objects for sexual excitement), tranvestism (cross-dressing by a heterosexual male), pedophilia (real or imagined sexual activity with a child), exhibitionism (exposing the genitals to a stranger) and voyeurism (observation of other people undressing, naked or engaged in sexual activity) are all also classed as paraphilias.

Persistent inhibition of sexual desire, excitement or orgasm, along with certain functional disorders, form the third group, the psychosexual dysfunctions. The fourth group includes ego-dystonic homosexuality, in which the individual states that he or she has been persistently distressed by homosexual arousal in spite of a desire to initiate or maintain heterosexual relationships.

Factitious Disorders and Disorders of Impulse Control

Disorders in the first of these categories are characterized by symptoms — physical or psychological — produced under voluntary control. Typically an individual pretends to be ill, in a compulsive way, but the deceit is not discovered and he or she repeatedly assumes the role of a "patient". Disorders of impulse control include pathological gambling (to the detriment of personal or family life), kleptomania (a compulsive impulse to steal), pyromania (a compulsion to set fires) and explosive disorder (recurrent loss of control leading to assault or damage to property).

Personality Disorders

The final major category in the *DSM–III* breakdown consists of various disorders of personality

that are not severe enough to be regarded as psychotic. Pervasive mistrust or suspicion of other people, with hypersensitivity, is characteristic of paranoid personality disorder. The individual usually lacks a true sense of humor and often expects to be the subject of a threat or trickery; he or she may question the loyalty of others or be pathologically jealous. An individual with schizoid personality disorder is indifferent to the feelings of others and fails to form social relationships. One with schizotypal personality disorder, on the other hand, displays "oddness" in thought and perception, such as magical thinking ("a sixth sense") and illusions, sometimes with strange speech and social isolation.

Histrionic personality disorder is defined in terms of overdramatic and intense behavior, in which the individual plays a role to gain attention. A low boredom threshold is typical. The key feature of narcissistic personality disorder is an inflated sense of self-importance, with a need for constant attention and success. Antisocial personality disorder involves prolonged antisocial behavior, often with aggression and criminality.

Hypersensitivity to possible rejection by others is an essential feature of avoidant personality disorder, in which the individual has low self-esteem and withdraws from society. In dependent personality disorder, the individual lacks self-confidence and allows someone else to virtually run his or her life, never making any major decisions. People with compulsive personality disorder find it difficult to be generous with their possessions or emotions, want their own way, and are often overcommitted to work. Finally, passive-aggressive personality disorder is characterized by a reluctance to perform adequately (at work or socially), often manifest as procrastination or intentional "forgetfulness."

Treating Mental Disorders

There are several approaches to helping the mentally ill. Some therapies focus on unconscious motives, others on subjective feelings, and still others on actual behaviors. Some therapies are biological in nature — such as shock therapy and drug therapy. They are aimed at chemical disturbance and can be quite effective for a number of problems from panic attacks to major depression. There are also various types of individual psychotherapy aimed at giving the patient insight into personal problems or more appropriate coping strategies. Among these are brief (twelve to twenty sessions) therapies and more long-term traditional insight-oriented psychotherapies. Various group psychotherapies, including play therapy, psychodrama and social skills training, may also be used. Behavior therapy, on the other hand, attempts to change behavior by eliminating undesirable behavior and learning desirable behaviors, without paying attention to motivation.

Essentially all the therapies (individual or group) can be traced back to three great intellectual traditions: the behavioral, psychoanalytic and humanistic models. The behavioral model — using behavior therapy techniques such as desensitization or successive approximation — assumes that maladaptive behavior is learned and persists because of the individual's learning history and current interactions with the environment. Treatment therefore uses an educational or training model because, just as maladaptive behavior is learned, it can be replaced by new adaptive behaviors.

The major focus of treatment is on the (measurable) change of some specific problem or source of

distress. Behavior therapists may attempt to assess and modify a patient's behavior in his or her natural setting as well as in the consulting room or hospital. Behavior treatments are adapted and tailored for the patient, so that all well-established procedures are molded to each patient's needs. Each treatment is considered as an experiment in specifying objective goals and measuring progress during treatment.

The psychoanalytic and psychodynamic models include a diverse variety of approaches which have in common the belief that unconscious wishes and fears shape behavior. It may be supportive or insight-oriented. Psychoanalysis — as developed by Sigmund Freud — was originally aimed at the discovery and resolution of repressed impulses. It recognized that they are the residue of childhood wishes and fears, defenses against which give rise to conflict. The patient is encouraged to freely-associate by talking about whatever comes to mind, such as early life, recent dreams, constant fears, problems at work. But because nothing happens at random, patterns of defense and conflict will emerge. The therapist offers interpretation that must be perspicacious, properly timed and at the appropriate depth. The goal is insight into the origins and causes of specific problem

behaviors, and its generalization to various new experiences.

The other psychodynamic therapies may differ according to the developmental periods (for example, early childhood versus adolescence), motivational factors (for example, sex versus power) or other properties they emphasize. Nevertheless, nearly all of them share the attributes described.

The humanistic therapies, more popular in the 1960s than currently, are characteristically optimistic, attempting to help people realize their potential. They usually emphasize the formation of a warm, empathic therapeutic relationship from which the client can derive a sense of the therapist's unconditional positive regard. They generally use a non-directive, client-centered approach, which focuses on the precise reflection and clarification of the meaning of the client's own statements. Existential psychotherapies focus on the individual's attainment of a sense of personal identity and responsibility for his or her actions in the world. There are various forms of group therapy that have adapted principles of humanistic psychology to the group setting.

Although every treatment claims particular success, systemic outcome studies generally show that all therapies produce more benefit than no treatment at all. In addition, some treatments have been found to be especially effective for particular disorders. For instance, behavior therapy is particularly good at dealing with phobias, whereas psychodynamic theories are helpful in dealing with some forms of guilt, or with personality disorders. Brief therapies can be effective in dealing with well circumscribed focal problems.

Influencing Motivation at Work

How can workers be motivated? Are open-planned offices more efficient than old-fashioned "private" offices? What is the optimal organizational structure? For more than eighty years, industrial psychologists have been intrigued by questions of behavior at work, especially the problem of how to motivate workers.

In 1939, a now classic study of the industrial environment was conducted by the Americans Roethlisberger and Dickinson. In the Hawthorne plant of the Western Electric Company, just out-

The intriguing, mood-changing potential of color has long been part of folklore, and is now becoming a legitimate field of study for color engineers. Their researches indicate that violet induces melancholy; red thirst (which is perhaps the reason behind the red decor of many a bar); and blue a feeling of relaxation. Indeed, old people are said to get ''blue thirsty'' as their yellowing eye fluids filter out blue light. Yellow, by contrast, gives rise to optimism and energy; orange stimulates the appetite; and an appeal for charity is most likely to be successful if it arrives through the mail sealed in a light blue-green envelope.

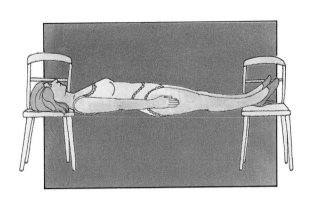

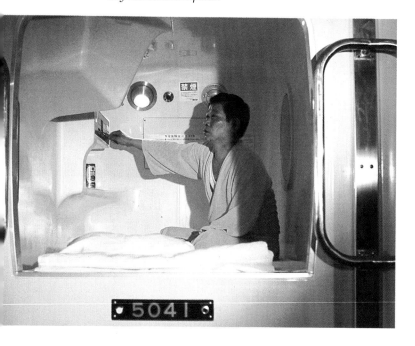

Guests hunker down for the night at a Japanese hotel in capsules designed to take up the minimum amount of space. Crowded urban conditions are a source of stress about which many city-dwellers complain.

side Chicago, a group of female workers were placed in a test room in which the level of illumination was varied up or down in a systematic manner. The results were rather odd: productivity increased but in a pattern that could not be correlated with the level of illumination. The workers' output remained high even when the illumination level was reduced to that of moonlight.

Thirteen different work factors were further varied and their effects on productivity recorded. These included length of rest pauses, length of work day, and work week, method of payment, place of work, the provision of a free lunch, and so on. Productivity increased with almost every change of work conditions. Even when subjects were returned to the initial, standard conditions that existed at the start of the research, productivity continued to rise. These findings were replicated several times, with different tasks, different groups of workers, and in different settings.

The answer is simple but nevertheless important. The women in this factory knew that they were being observed and reacted favorably to the special attention that they received and to the relatively free supervisory climate in the test room. And it was the interest of the researchers rather than any of the numerous physical changes that caused the change in behavior. It has become called the "Hawthorne effect."

This was to be the beginning of the human relations school of organizational psychology. This school of thought is based on the premise that the need for recognition, security, and sense of belonging is more important in determining workers' morale and productivity than the physical conditions under which they work. Worker complaints were redefined, not necessarily as an objective recital of facts, but rather as a symptom of individual status problems. The role of social demands from both inside and outside the work plant in conditioning worker attitudes and effectiveness was appreciated. The role of informal groups within the work plant in exercising strong social controls over the work habits and attitudes of the individual worker was also recognized.

The question of motivation raises the difficult but interesting question of the relationship between job satisfaction and productivity. Three possible relationships occur. Firstly, job satisfaction could cause (or lead to) increased productivity. Most people believe this to be true, namely that contented workers with high morale tend to work well. Frequently, in industrial studies, the relationship between satisfaction and productivity has been found to be weak. It is entirely possible that a satisfied worker could like his work and his fellow workers so well that his productivity would be adversely affected by frequent conversation. On the other hand, a dissatisfied worker might be extremely productive in order to progress to a more satisfying position or because of fear of his supervisor, losing his job, or another reason.

Secondly, high productivity can lead to rewards which in turn lead to satisfaction. It may be true that when people are rewarded specifically for their effort and ability, they tend to be satisfied. Similarly, it may be true that when reward is not specifically related to performance level (such as a Christmas bonus for all employees), satisfaction is not likely to occur.

Thirdly, of course, there could be a situation in which both or neither are true. That is, satisfaction may sometimes cause productivity, and productivity may sometimes cause satisfaction. Satisfaction and productivity may sometimes be unrelated.

The more crowded the world becomes, the more difficult it is for an individual to stamp an identity on society. People are as liable to experience feelings of alienation within a throng as in solitude.

Other variables may intervene in these relationships. Group sentiments may have a very powerful effect which changes this relationship. For example, a satisfied worker may be influenced by his work group to restrict production if the organization does not respond with significant changes. A dissatisfied worker, by contrast, may be highly productive if the attitude of the work group is such that high performance is the accepted behavior of the work group as a whole.

Influence Via the Media

How effective are the television, radio and newspapers at manipulating the mind? Do television programs about violence, for example, increase the likelihood that viewers will become violent? By contrast, do programs showing prosocial, altruistic behavior promote goodness? Or does the portrayal of men and women in their traditional roles (doctors are nearly always men, nurses are nearly always women) perpetuate stereotyped sex roles? One of the ways in which nondemocratic governments attempt to prevent criticism and public debate is through strict control of the media and

what it broadcasts. And does such control work?

Firstly, how pervasive is the influence of the media? Recent statistics have shown that almost every household in the United States has at least one television. On average, the set is turned on for almost six hours per day. Both adults and children see more than three hours per day. Around forty per cent of all leisure time is devoted to television, and, after sleep and work, television is the greatest consumer of time.

In the 1970s, eighty per cent of American television programs and ninety per cent of children's shows contained some violence. Between the ages of five and fifteen, a young viewer may witness the violent death of about 13,000 people on the television screen! Various studies have been done — using different experimental techniques — to examine the effects of portraying antisocial behavior on television programs.

Many sensational anecdotes have been reported in the popular press concerning people imitating what they have seen on the television. One Los Angeles seven-year-old put ground glass in the family meal, just as he had seen it done on the TV.

Within a few days of a television program depicting a bank raid in which robbers threatened to detonate bombs they had attached to themselves, five separate robberies of this sort were reported in Los Angeles, despite the fact that no incident of this kind had ever been reported before. However, these idiosyncratic cases cannot be taken as proof of a general phenomenon.

More systematic investigations have shown a link between violent television and antisocial behavior. In one study, two groups of adolescent male juvenile delinquents living in group cottages were carefully assessed for aggressive behavior, such as physical threats, verbal aggression, assaults, and wanton destruction of inanimate objects, over a period of three weeks. Then the boys in one cottage were exposed to five violent movies over a one-week period, while boys in another cottage saw only nonviolent films. Those who saw the violent movies showed a significant increase in most types of aggression over their original rate, whereas the nonviolent movie watchers did not.

Some have argued the precise opposite — that watching violence "gets it out of your system." This is the so-called vicarious catharsis hypothesis, which argues that seeing others' distress drains off one's own unhappiness, or that reading pornography reduces the probability that the reader will be motivated to carry out sexual attacks rather than increases it.

Various attempts have been made to test this theory. They usually involve getting two groups of people and angering one group (usually by insulting them) but not the other. Then half of each group (angered and non-angered) are shown violent television movies, while the other half of each group see nonviolent films. After that, all the volunteers are given the opportunity to give electric shocks to the person who insulted them. Several studies have shown that regardless of how much anger was aroused, people who saw violent movies deliver more shocks than subjects who saw nonviolent movies; that anger-aroused people respond more violently; and that angered volunteers who witness aggression respond most aggressively of all. There thus seems to be little support for the vicarious catharsis idea.

Glossary

adrenal glands endocrine glands located on top of the kidneys which release epinephrine when stimulated.

affectionless characters emotionally cold people who were given no opportunity to form attachments in infancy.

aggression forceful verbal or physical action by one party, either human or animal, with the intention of dominating another.

agoraphobia irrational fear of open spaces, possibly leading eventually to an inability to go out of doors at all.

altruism generosity to the point of selflessness or even self-sacrifice.

American sign language a system of communication that involves neither hearing nor lip-reading. Instead the hands are used to signify words or letters of the alphabet. Some other countries use different sign language systems.

amnesia loss of memory.

androgens male sex hormones.

antidepressant drug a drug prescribed to elevate the mood of a patient.

antipsychotic drug a drug prescribed to reduce psychotic symptoms.

anxiety a mixture of subjective and physiological events associated with stressful apprehension evoked by any threatening situation.

arousal the state of mental alertness in an individual which to some extent governs perceptual input and cognitive efficiency of behavior.

assertiveness the aspect of social behavior in which people or animals stand up for their own rights.

attachment figure a person who is looked to by an offspring for security and affection.

authoritarian tending to use the power of authority or strength rather than coercion or the ties of affection.

autogenic psychotherapy a method of treating patients suffering from stress, making them relax by focusing on qualities of different parts of the body.

behaviorism a school of psychology which emphasizes the roles of learning and environment in changes in behavior; the study of behavior in which only visible and measurable changes are considered acceptable.

behavior therapy a method of treatment within the behaviorist tradition; for example, modeling, in which there is an emphasis on observable events rather than underlying causes.

biofeedback method of obtaining information through electronic apparatus that permits a person to monitor his or her own physiological processes, usually by presenting a light or sound to indicate a rate or level, for example the heart rate and blood pressure.

Broca's area a portion of the left hemisphere of the brain under the temple which is involved in processing speech.

categorical perception the tendency to place a range of physical stimuli into categories; for example, light of a certain narrow band of wavelengths representing a number of slightly different shades may all be called red.

catharsis in psychoanalytic theory, a discharge of emotion which relieves anxiety.

classical conditioning a basic form of learning in which a neural stimulus elicits a reflex response as a result of its having for some time been combined with an external stimulus; sometimes called Pavlovian conditioning after its discoverer.

cognition psychological processes together amounting to awareness, such as perceiving, thinking, attending and remembering.

cognitive psychotherapy a method of treating patients suffering from neurotic complaints which focuses on the rearrangements of their statements of thoughts, memories and ideas.

compulsion an inescapable need to perform an action — sometimes an irrational one — generally repeatedly, and usually against the actor's will.

concrete operations stage the third of Piaget's developmental periods (from about seven to eleven years old) when a child begins to think in a framework of time and space, and is able to understand how others feel.

conditioned response in classical conditioning, the learned (but automatic) response to an external stimulus which was not initially evoked by that stimulus.

contingency in psychology experiments, the predictable availability of a reward following a particular response, basic for example to teaching animals to do things.

convergent thinking constructive, logical, sequential reasoning.

cornea transparent membrane forming the front of the eyeball.

correlation a statistical index of predictability, indicating how predictable two associated events or measurements are in relation to each other: +1 indicates perfect positive predictability; 0 indicates no predictability; and −1 indicates a perfect negative relationship.

creativity original and constructive thinking.

credibility the believability of an individual or event.

crossmodal perception the coordination by the mind of the responses of the various senses; for example, the way in which the shape of an object can be visualized when it has been touched, not seen.

crystallized intelligence accumulated knowledge.

deep structure in linguistics, the true meaning of a sentence, which may differ through associations and the use of figures of speech such as euphemism from its surface structure.

defense mechanism an adjustment of perception. It is usually made unconsciously, to reduce anxiety and conflict.

delusion unshakable belief that something is the case when it is not. An example is delusions of persecution, a certainty that one is being subjected to harassment.

denial an unconscious defense mechanism used to reduce conflict and anxiety by ignoring thoughts and feelings which are consciously intolerable.

depression strong, persistent feelings of gloom, discouragement and rejection, which may have physical concomitants, such as loss of appetite or weight, and which may have a biochemical basis.

discriminative stimulus a stimulus effective when a particular conditioning situation is in force; for example, the appearance of a red light making a car driver stop.

dishabituation the return of a response in its original strength once the effect of habituation to a stimulus is lost.

divergent thinking problem-solving method that involves generating numerous potentially constructive but diverse possibilities; sometimes called lateral thinking.

ectomorph a person with a tall, frail body frame, sometimes stereotyped as having a nervous and detached personality.

ego in Freud's psychoanalytic theory, that part of personality which consciously and rationally deals with reality.

egocentric describes a person who is self-oriented and thus unable to see another's point of view.

eidetic imagery a memory of visual images which is so detailed as to be like a photograph; photographic memory.

electroencephalogram (EEG) a recording of electrical activity in the brain derived from electrodes on the surface of the head.

emotion a general state of mind involving a mood; for example being happy, sad, angry or fearful. Many such emotions have physical effects on the body.

encoding the act of organizing material to be remembered in certain forms; for example, acoustic encoding organizes data by sound properties.

encounter group a method of therapy in which small groups meet regularly to improve their social sensitivity, creative ability or perceptual awareness.

endomorph a person with a short, fat body frame, sometimes stereotyped as a jolly and self-indulgent personality.

estrogens female sex hormones, partly responsible for female secondary sexual characteristics.

ethology a branch of psychobiology which focuses on animal behavior and its evolution.

epinephrine a hormone, secreted by the adrenal glands, which arouses the body for action; also called adrenaline.

equity theory a theory concerning work satisfaction that focuses on the exchange of energy and feedback for a worker.

extrovert a type of person who is outgoing, interested in other people and in social activities.

fluid intelligence problem-solving capability.

formal operations stage the fourth of Piaget's developmental periods (from about twelve years old onward) when a person is able to think abstractly.

functional psychosis mental illness which has no presently known physical basis; for example, schizophrenia.

genius a person with exceptional mental ability; an IQ of 145 or more is sometimes used as a criterion.

generalization thought process resulting in the formation of a concept.

glucocorticoids hormones secreted by the adrenal glands which increase the availability of energy (blood sugar).

habituation a state of mind in which a conscious response to a stimulus eventually ceases after the stimulus has been presented repeatedly.

hallucination a sensory experience, usually auditory or visual, that has no external stimulus.

hormones substances secreted mainly by the endocrine glands that stimulate the body to activity of various kinds; examples include estrogens and epinephrine.

hypochondria exaggerated concern for one's own health.

hypnosis an induced dreamlike state in which a person is relatively relaxed and susceptible to suggestion by the hypnotist.

hypothalamus a small structure located above the brainstem that is involved in the control of certain behavior; the lateral (sides) and ventromedial (mid-front) regions are important in the regulation of food intake.

hysterical or histrionic, describes a personality type characterized by excitability and attention-seeking behavior. It is associated with conversion reactions, in which the patient exhibits physical symptoms (such as paralysis) that have no organic cause.

id in Freud's psychoanalytic theory, the unconscious and instinctual wishes.

imprinting the choice of an attachment figure or object during a very short critical period soon after birth.

intelligence the ability to think abstractly, to learn from experience and use information, and to adapt to changes.

intonation pattern of inflection in speech, over a whole sentence or within a phrase or even a single word.

introvert a type of person who is self-reliant, possibly a loner, who has no particular need to be with other people.

IQ intelligence quotient, a score on an intelligence test in which the average score is 100; various factors, such as age, are taken into account. Whether intelligence can really be measured, however, remains controversial.

kleptomania a compulsion to steal.

learning usable memory; a concept or concepts adopted permanently or

153

semipermanently as a result of experience.

lens a structure in the eye capable of focusing light rays onto the retina at the back of the eye.

limbic system a set of midbrain structures involved in motivational and emotional behavior, including hunger, thirst and sleep.

long-term memory an organizational mode of memory by which material is stored from a few minutes to years at a time.

mainstreaming in education, the practice of mixing students who have some disability or handicap with ordinary students.

manic depression mental illness characterized by extreme shifts in emotion, including elation (manic phase) and despondency (depressive phase).

mastery learning an educational method in which course objectives are clearly specified and all students are expected to learn all the material.

mental illness any lasting disorder involving the mind which disrupts the smooth conduct of life.

mesomorph a person with a muscular, athletic body frame, sometimes stereotyped as a confident, likable and helpful friend.

modeling a method of training in which the learner is shown complex behavior in order to imitate it; observational learning.

mood a persistent disposition of the mind toward a specific dominating feeling, such as elation or depression.

motivation the reason, intention or force behind behavior which seeks to reduce needs or achieve goals.

neurosis an imprecise term for a mental disorder in which a person is unable to cope with anxiety and stress, and develops subjective discomfort and often symptoms.

niche the status that an animal has reached within its environment through evolutionary adaptation.

nonverbal communication communicating with others by means of gestures and manners that do not involve any form of words, spoken, written or signed; for example, making eye contact.

noun phrase a unit of grammar that contains a noun and any qualifying adjectives and articles; for example, a black horse.

object permanence the perception of objects as real, enduring fixtures in the world; children achieve this level of understanding during their first year.

obsession a persistent unwanted and irrational idea which intrudes into daily life.

organic psychosis a mental illness (psychosis) arising from identifiable physical damage to the brain.

paranoid overly suspicious. At an extreme it describes elaborate systems of persecutory thought based on misreading of reality, and in even more extreme cases on delusions and hallucinations.

perceptual constancy the fact that a physical attribute of a stimulus does not seem to change despite a change in the pattern of stimulation reaching the senses; for example, a tree appears to be the same height no matter how far away it is; this is called size constancy.

perceptual illusion a situation in which people agree that the characteristics of a stimulus appear different from what they actually are.

personality the relatively permanent characteristics of behavior that make one individual different from others.

phobia intense, constant, irrational fear of an object or situation, for example a spider or elevators.

phoneme the smallest pronounceable unit of speech which differentiates the meaning of words; a sound that can be represented by a single symbol in phonetic script.

preoperational stage the second of Piaget's developmental periods (from about two to six years old) when the child realizes he or she is separate from the world and is able to imagine objects and events in other forms; for example, that clay can be shaped into either a ball or a snakelike form.

prosocial behavior positive social behavior, such as generosity and altruism, both of which benefit others.

psychoanalysis the theoretical view and therapeutic practice developed by Sigmund Freud which stresses that unconscious mechanisms are responsible for behavior.

psychodynamic pertaining to behavior in relation to competing motivations, especially in Freud's psychoanalytic theory.

psycholinguistics the study of the psychological aspects of language and language learning.

psychosis a severe mental disorder in which a person is out of touch with reality.

psychosomatic describing physical complaints and symptoms that are aggravated by psychological stress; for example, some types of headaches.

psychotherapy any method of treatment designed to alleviate emotional and behavioral disorders.

pyromania a compulsion to start fires.

reflex an involuntary, rapid behavioral response mediated by a two-nerve arc. For example, blinking when an object is suddenly presented close to the face.

repression a defense mechanism by which an undesirable or distressing memory or feeling is excluded from consciousness.

retina the cells at the back of the eye in which sensations of light are changed into nerve impulses.

reinforcement an event or events serving to strengthen the link between a stimulus and a response; for example, a positive reinforcement may be a reward, and a negative reinforcement may be a punishment.

retrieval the process by which a memory is brought back to the conscious mind.

ritual behavior following a rigidly set

pattern or procedure.

schedule of reinforcement the sequence by which positive or negative reinforcement follows a response according to a systematic rule — for example, after every fifth response.

schema a person's general ideas about future events and ambitions.

schizophrenia a type of mental illness, of duration greater than six months, in which there are major disturbances of thought, perception, emotion and behavior, usually including hallucinations and delusions at some time.

secondary reinforcer the reward or punishment that the conditioned response following a discriminative stimulus itself eventually represents.

self-concept an individual's awareness of the combination of attributes and behaviors that make him or her unique.

self-esteem the value at which an individual assesses himself or herself; for example, in high self-esteem there is a positive attitude toward self.

semantics the study of the deep structure of sentences, the true meaning of communication.

sensory deprivation the enforced absence of all stimulatory experience, resulting in loss of the ability to concentrate and feeling of insecurity and nausea.

sensory threshold the level of sensory experience at which a tiny sensation (touch, taste, smell or whatever) just becomes detectable by an individual.

sensorimotor stage the first of Piaget's developmental periods (from birth to eighteen months) when a child comes to understand object permanence.

separation anxiety the distress shown by an infant when no attachment figure is present.

shaping a process of sequential conditioning in order to achieve a complex operant response that would not occur spontaneously; it can be effected by progressively rewarding those responses that approximate successively more to the full required response.

social skills in the behaviorist tradition, aspects of interpersonal behavior that are a topic of study or training.

socialization the process by which a child learns to take his or her place in society.

split-brain operation surgery in which part of the connection between the hemispheres of the brain is severed, sometimes used to help severe epileptics.

stereotype to assign an individual to a specific notional category on the grounds of sex, race, physical characteristics, social standing or some criterion other than the individual's own personal qualities.

stranger anxiety the distress shown by an infant when an unfamiliar person is present, usually seen in infants between eight and twelve months old.

stress a state of anxiety in which an individual feels pressurized by the events of life.

subliminal perception perception without awareness.

superego in Freud's psychoanalytic theory, the part of personality which embodies conscience and moral standards.

superstitious response a response that occurs because it has fortuitously been reinforced in the past.

supraliminal sensation perceptual stimulus that is sufficiently strong for a perceiver to be aware of it.

systematic desensitization a method

of psychotherapy in which the patient is confronted with a graded sequence of anxiety-provoking situations, possibly in conjunction with relaxation training.

temperament the combination of relatively enduring characteristics or traits that describe a person — for example, happy, adaptable and regular; a temperament is believed to have some biological basis.

tranquilizers drugs used to reduce anxiety on a temporary basis.

transformation in Chomsky's theory of language, the rules that govern how a sentence may correctly change form to alter the sense; for example, to change a statement into a question.

transformational grammar Chomsky's theory of language in which semantic meaning is transformed (following the rules of transformation) into actual sentences.

unconscious the part of the mind that is below the level of consciousness; according to some psychological theory, it may be a repository for "unwanted" or unpleasant memories.

verb phrase a unit of grammar that contains a verb and any qualifying adverbs; it commonly corresponds to the predicate — all of a sentence except its subject — and may thus also contain a noun phrase.

verbal ability the ability to use language, including reading and writing.

visual cliff an apparatus used to test the depth perception of animals or human babies.

visuospatial ability the ability to perform tasks involving geometric manipulation; for example, completing three-dimensional jigsaw puzzles.

vocal tract the cavities above the larynx, including the mouth and nasal space, which are used to vary speech sounds.

Illustration Credits

Introduction
6, *The Ancient of Days* by William Blake/Whitworth Art Gallery, University of Manchester.

What is the mind?
8, Michael Holford/Wellcome Collection. 10, *Jesus Healing the Man of Unclean Spirit*/Hessisches Landesmuseum, Darmstadt/Bridgeman Art Library. 11, Detail from *The Temptation of St Anthony*, Isenheim Altarpiece by Grünewald/Unterlinden Museum, Colmar/Giraudon/Bridgeman Art Library. 12, Michael Holford/Science Museum, London. 13, Science Photo Library. 14 (left), Popperfoto. 14 (right), Alexander Tsiaras/Science Photo Library. 15, **Rob Shone**. 16, Benser/Zefa. 17, Archives of the History of American Psychology, Akron University, Ohio. 18 (left), **Mick Saunders**. 18 (right), Rodney Bond/Zefa. 19 (top), Mary Evans Picture Library. 19 (bottom), *Punch* Magazine. 20, Jennie Woodcock. 21 (top), Mike Dixon/Photoresources. 21 (bottom), United Artists/Kobal Collection. 22, *Cygnus Atratus* from Ornithological and Zoological Works by John Gould/Christie's, London/Bridgeman Art Library. 23 (top), **Mick Saunders**. 23 (bottom), Fotomarket/Zefa. 24, **Rob Shone**. 25, Alfred Gescheidt/Imagebank. 26, Damm/Zefa. 27 (left), Acorn. 27 (right), Barnaby's Picture Library. 28, Science Photo Library. 29, Steenmans/Zefa. 30, Murray/Zefa. 31, Mary Evans Picture Library.

The Developing Mind
32, Zefa. 34, Petit Format/Nestle/Steiner/Science Photo Library. 35, H. Mueller/Zefa. 36 (left), T. G. Allen. 36 (right), **Mick Gillah**. 37, **Rob Shone**. 38, Tim Woodcock. 39, Jennie Woodcock. 40, **Shirley Willis**. 41, **Shirley Willis**. 42, Stockphotos. 43, M. L. du Dohna/Zefa. 44, Jennie Woodcock. 45, Jennie Woodcock. 46, Michael McIntyre/Camerapix Hutchison. 47 (left), University of Wisconsin Primate Laboratory. 47 (right), University of Wisconsin Primate Laboratory. 48, Jennie Woodcock. Foldout, (outside) Zefa, (inside) **Mick Gillah**. 49 (top), Mary Evans Picture Library. 49 (bottom), **Mick Gillah**. 50 (top), Rod and Moira Borland/Survival Anglia. 50 (bottom), Jennie Woodcock. 51, Warner Brothers/Kobal Collection. 52, **Mick Gillah**. 53 (top), Carroll Seghers/Stockphotos. 53 (bottom), Popperfoto. 54, New School for Social Research, New York. 55, **Mick Gillah**. 56, *Punch* Magazine. 57, Jennie Woodcock. 58, Jennie Woodcock. 59, Norbert Schafer/Imagebank.

Thinking and Learning
60, R. Bond/Zefa. 62, Food and Wine from France. 63, **Mick Saunders**. 64 (top), **Mick Saunders**. 64 (bottom), Ivan Strasburg/Camerapix Hutchison. 65, **Mick Saunders**. 66, **Mick Saunders**. 67, *Cirkellimiet IV 1960 Heaven and Hell* by M. C. Escher/Haags Gemeentemuseum, Den Haag, Netherlands. 68, Mary Evans Picture Library. 69, Popperfoto. 70, **Mick Gillah**. 71, **Mick Gillah**. 72, **Shirley Willis**. 73, P. Turner/

Imagebank. 74, Mary Evans Picture Library. 75, Zefa. 76, **Shirley Willis**. 77, Armstrong/Zefa. 78, Tim Woodcock. 79 (top), Archives of the History of American Psychology, Akron University, Ohio. 79 (bottom), Archives of the History of American Psychology, Akron University, Ohio. 80, Michael McIntyre/Camerapix Hutchison. 81, Archives of the History of American Psychology, Akron University, Ohio. 82, H. Buchner/Zefa. 83, Camerapix Hutchison. 84, Toby Seger/Imagebank. 85, Paramount/Kobal Collection. 86, Jennie Woodcock. 87, Acorn.

A Meeting of Minds
88, Detail from *The Tower of Babel* by Pieter Breughel/Kunsthistorisches Museum, Vienna. 90, **Mick Gillah**. 91, **Mick Gillah**. 92, **Chris Rose**. 93, Jack Baker/Imagebank. 94 (top), Richter/Barnaby's Picture Library. 94 (bottom), C. Hackmann/Zefa. 95, Camerapix Hutchison. 96, Tony Stone. 97, Camerapix Hutchison. 98, Kobal Collection. 99, **Aziz Khan**. 100, Vision Aid Systems. 101, Jorg Trobzsch/Zefa. 102, **Mick Saunders**. 103, Cable and Wireless.

The Hidden Self
104, Michael Holford. 106, M. di Giacomo/Imagebank. 107, **Rob Shone**. 108 (left), Blumebild/Zefa. 108 (right), Paramount/Kobal Collection. 109, *A Good Meal* by Thomas Rowlandson/Private Collection/Bridgeman Art Library. 110, Blume/Zefa. 111, **Mick Gillah**. 112 (left), Blok/Zefa. 112 (right), Richard House/Camerapix Hutchison. 113, **Yann le Goaec**. 114, **Mick Gillah**. 115 (top), Michael McIntyre/Camerapix Hutchison. 115 (bottom), Stockphotos. 116, Donald E. Carroll/Imagebank. 117, Alfred Gescheidt/Imagebank. 118, Roy Hunt/Survival Anglia. 119 (top), Stockphotos. 119 (bottom), Juliet Highet/Camerapix Hutchison. 120, **Rob Shone**. 121, Owenbank. 122, Sue Harrison. 123, The Adlerian Society of Great Britain.

Modifying Behavior
124, T. Craddock/Zefa. 126, Imperial War Museum, London. 127, Dr. Hanz Kramarz/Zefa. 129, Voss/Zefa. 130, Imperial War Museum, London. 131, John P. Kelly/Imagebank. 132, Mary Evans Picture Library. 133, **Shirley Willis**. 134, Mary Evans Picture Library. 135, Michael Holford/Estall. 136, B. Croxford/Zefa. 137, William D. Adams/Imagebank. 138, **Mick Saunders**. 139, Max Munn Autra/Kobal Collection. 140, Leslie Woodhead/Camerapix Hutchison. 141 (top), Bill Coward/Barnaby's Picture Library. 141 (bottom), Camerapix Hutchison. 142, National Library of Medicine, Maryland. 143, **Rob Shone**. 144, NASA. 145, Zefa. 146, H. Bombrowski/Zefa. 147, **Rob Shone**. 148, Michael McIntyre/Camerapix Hutchison. 149, Jennie Woodcock. 150, Universal/Kobal Collection. 151, *Cupid Delivering Psyche* by Sir Edward Burne-Jones/Sheffield Art Gallery/Bridgeman Art Library.

Index

Page numbers in bold type indicate illustrations and photographs

A

ability, general factor of, 18, 32, 83, 115
  language learning, 98
  motor, **39**, 41–43, **43**
  social, 43
  verbal, 18, 27, 55, 86, 93
  visuo-spatial, 14, 18, 34–36, **39**, 55, 86, 93
abnormality, mental, 23–26
abuse, drug, 26, 139
accent, regional, 95
Adler, Alfred, 21, 123
Adler: *Practice and Theory of Individual Psychology*, 123
adolescence, mental disorders of, 136
adrenal gland, **111**, 117
adrenocorticotropic hormone (ACTH), **111**
advertising, 129, **129**, 130, **131**, 132
  subliminal, 130–134
affective disorder, 140
aggression, 49, 55, 105–107, **107**, 110, 151
aggressiveness, 20, 145
agoraphobia, 113, 141
alcohol, 138, **146**
alpha rhythm, **84**
Alzheimer's disease, 138
American Naturalist, The, 81
American Psychiatric Association, 136
American Sign Language, 93
Ames, Adelbert, 64
amnesia, 138
  retrograde, 75
  psychogenic, 144
amphetamine, 26, 138
Anaxagoras, 9
androgen, 108
anesthesia, hysterical, 24
anger, 129
angina, 117
anorexia nervosa, 137
anti-androgen, 108
antisocial personality disorder, 145
anxiety, **25**, 110, **112**, 114–115, **119**, 129
  disorder, 136, 140–141
  effects of, 114
  free-floating, 77
ape, 92
appetite, 109–110, **109**, **110**
"archetype", 21
Aristotle, 9
arm, 41
arousal, emotional, **112**
  physical, 110, 113, 118
art, 6
artery, **119**
  coronary, 117
articulation disorder, 137

assimilation, theory of, 43
association, learning by, 98
astrology, **14**
atheroma, 117
attachment, 46–48, **47**
  figure, 45
attention deficit disorder, 136
auditory system of mammal, 95
auditory threshold, 36
autism, infantile, 137
autogenic training, 118
autohypnosis, 118
avoidance anxiety disorder, 136
avoidance behavior, 141
avoidance response, 70
avoidant personality disorder, 145

B

barbiturates, 138
Barron, Frank, 84
Bartlett, Frederic, 77
Beatty, Geoff, 98
Beck, Aaron, 120
bed-wetting, 137
bee, dance of, 89
behavior, **32**, 33, 36, 40, **40**, 47, 48, 50, 66, 68, 69, **71**
  change, 86
  illness, 136
  physiological factor in, 52
  stress b., 72
  therapy, 119, 145–146
behaviorism, 15, 16, **16**
Bem, Daryl, 113
Benson, Dr. Herbert, 118
Berkeley, George, 10
Binet, Alfred, **79**, 83
biofeedback, 119
birdsong, 90
Blake, William, 7
Blake: *The Ancient of Days*, **7**
blood, circulation of, 12, 69, 117
  sugar, 109, **111**
  transport of hormones by, 108, **111**
body fluids, supposed influence of, 10
body image, **108**
body/mind interaction, 12, 15
bondage, 144
Boring's wife/mother-in-law, 62
boy, 55–56
brain, 6, 13, 14, 23, 26, 63, 64, 109, 110, **111**, 117
  activity, chemical, **13**, 14
  activity, electrical, 13, 14, 28, **28**, **84**
  activity, electrical, in infant, 30
  control of aggression, 106, **107**
  damage, 13, 49
  development, **34**
  electronic, 80
  function, 14
  growth, **34**
  hemisphere, 27, 93

language function, 27, 93
  malfunction, 6
  response to sexual stimulus, 108
  scan, **14**
brainstem, 36
Brazetton, T. Berry, 45
breathing, 117
Broca, Pierre Paul, 93–94
Broca's area, 94
Bruner, Jerome, 54
Bruner: *Processes of Cognitive Growth*, 54
Bruner, Oliver and Greenfield: *Studies in Cognitive Growth*, 54
bulimia, 137

C

caffeine, 138
cancer, 116
cannabis, 138
castration, 108
catatonia, 139
Cattell, James McKeen, 18, 19, 81
central nervous system, 25, 139
cerebral cortex, 28, 69, **111**
Charcot, Jean, 24–25
Chess, Stella, 51
childhood, 20, **32**, 69
childhood disorders, mental, 136–137
children's books, 56, **57**
chimpanzee, facial expressions of, **92**
  language learning by, 90, 92
  ranking, 107
  stimulation of ch. hypothalamus, 107, **107**
chinchilla, 95
Chomsky, Noam, 27, 98, 100, 103
Church, 12
cocaine, 138
cognition, 27, 54, 73
color, **147**
communication, 9, 27, 89–103
  chimpanzee, 93
  dolphin, 93
  non-verbal, 90–91, **94**, 97–98
  parent-child, **99**
  primate, 97
  whale, 93
  use of computer in, **100**
communications, 6, 103, **103**
compulsion, 141
compulsive personality disorder, 145
computer, 27–28, 92
  -assisted teaching, 86, **87**
  language, **27**
  program for voice analysis, 96
  technology, analogy with, **15**
  use by partially-sighted, **100**
concentration, 24
concussion, 75
conditioned emotional response, 72
conditioned response, 68, 70, **71**
conditioning, classical, 16, 68, 70, **71**, 72

conditioning, operant, 16, 70, 71, 72, 86
conduct disorder, 136
consciousness, **13**, 35
consumer psychology, 128–129, **131**
conversion disorder, 143
cornea, 34
creativity, 6, 83–85, **83**, **85**
crowding, **148**, **149**
crying, 41
culture, 9
cyclothymic disorder, 140

D
Darwin, Charles, 13, 17
Darwin: *Expression of the Emotions in Man and Animals*, 13
deafness, detection of, 36
"death instinct", 20, 105–106
decision-making, 114, 115, 119
defense mechanism, 20
delirium, alcohol, 138
delusion, 24, 25, 121–122, **133**, 138–139
dementia, multi-infarct, 138
    praecox, *see* schizophrenia
    primary degenerative, 138
    senile, 24
demon, **10**
dependence, drug, 139
dependent personality disorder, 145
depersonalization disorder, 144
depression, **25**, 77, **112**, 114, **114**, **116**, **117**, **133**, 140, 145
    manic, 24, **133**
depth, perception of, 35
Descartes, René, 12
desensitization, 145
development, **32**, 33, 40
    auditory, 36–37
    cephalocaudal, 41
    cognitive, levels of, 54, 56, 58, 83
    evolutionary view of, 46–48
    intellectual, **40**, 43
    moral, 48
    motor, **39**, **40**, 41, 43
    physical, 40–43
    proximodistal, 43
    visual, 34–36, **39**
developmental articulation disorder, 137
developmental disorder, 137
devil, **10**
Diagnostic and Statistical Manual of Mental Disorders, 136
diet, 117
digestion, 69
"dimensions", 54
discipline, **115**
dishabituation, 68
dissociative disorder, 144
dolphin, 93, **93**
dopamine receptor, 25
dorsomedial nucleus, **107**

drawing, **82**
dream, 28, **28**, 30, **30**, 85, 137
drive state, 110
drug, **25**
    abuse, 26, 139
    anti-depressant, 25
    anti-depressant, tricyclic, 119
    amphetamine, abuse of, 26
    psychedelic, 26
    sedative, 25
    therapy, 145
dyslexia, 137
dysphoria, 140
dysthymic disorder, 140

E
ear, 34, 61
eating center, 109
eating disorder, 137
ectomorph, 53, 55, **55**
education, 69, 86–87
    pre-school, **86**
Ego, 20, **22**
eidetic imagery, 76
elective mutism, 136
electroconvulsive therapy (ECT), **117**
electroencephalogram (EEG), 28, **28**
elements, five, Taoist, 10
    four, Platonic, 10
Ellis, Albert, 120
Embedded Figures test, **52**
embryo, 33
emotion, 6, 15, **32**, 110, 112, **112**
emotionality, 51
encopresis, functional, 137
endocrine system, **111**
endomorph, 53, 55, **55**
enuresis, functional, 137
environment, 50, 65, **71**
    infant response to, 45–46, **47**
    influence of, in IQ, 80, 83
    influence of, on language learning, 27
enzyme, pancreatic, 69
epilepsy, 23, 85–86
epinephrine, **111**, 112, 116
Erikson, Erik, 142
Erikson: *Childhood and Society*, 142
Eros, 20
Escher: *Heaven and Hell*, 67
estrogen, 108
estrus, 108
evolution, 108
    theory of, 13, 14
evolutionary view of development, 46–48
exhibitionism, 144
exorcism, **10**
explosive disorder, 144
extroversion, **18**, 51
extrovert, 52, 53
eye, 34, 39, 61
    focus of, 34, 35

movement in newborn, 35
    pupil, 65
"eyebrow flash", 98, **98**
Eysenck, Hans, 18, **18**, 52, **53**

F
face, expression of, 98, **98**
    response of infant to, 34, **36**, **37**, 45
factitions disorders, 144
family, **24**
fats, 116
fear, 107, 110, 129, 140
feeding of infant, 43–44
Festinger, Leon, 126
fetishism, 144
fetus, 33
"fight or flight" reaction, 117
figure-ground reversal, **49**
focus, visual, 34, 35
free association, **24**
Freud, Anna, 142
Freud, Sigmund, 19, **19**, 20, **20**, 21, 28, 69, 105–106, 110, 120, 123, 134, 142, 146
Freud: *Interpretation of Dreams*, 28
Friedman and Rosenman, 117
frontal lobe, 94
fugue, psychogenic, 144
functional encopresis, 137
functional enuresis, 137
functionalism, 15

G
Galileo, 12, 17
Gall, Franz Josef, 15
Galton, Francis, 16, 18
gambling, pathological, 144
gastric secretion, 69
gene, 51, 53
"generative transformational grammar", 27
genetic factor in IQ, 80, 83
Gestalt psychology, **49**
gesture, **94**, 97
girl, 55–56
grammar, 98–103
    transformational rules of, 102–103, **102**
Gregory, Richard, 62
Grunewald: *The Temptation of St. Anthony*, 10

H
habituation, 68, 69
Hall, G. Stanley, 81
hallucination, 10, 24, 25, 66, 121, **122**, 138
    drug-induced, 26, 138

hand, 43
Harvey, William, 12
"Hawthorne effect", 148
head, 41
Head Start scheme, 80, 83, 87
healing, **10**
hearing, 34
   development of, 36–37
   impared, 36
heart, 12, 117, 118
   disease, coronary, 116, 117
hemisphere, 27, 85–86, 93
heredity, 16, 18
hermaphrodite, 55–56
higher nervous center, 34
Hippocrates, 12, 23
histrionic personality disorder, 145
homosexuality, ego-dystonic, 144
Hopkins, Gerard Manley, **7**
hormone, 28, 107, **111**, 117
   adrenal cortical, 117
   corticoid, **111**
   growth, **30**
   sex, 108
hospitalism, 45
hunger, 109
hyperactivity, 136, 140
   autonomic, 141
hyperthyroidism, 52
hypnosis, 24–25
hypochondriasis, 144
hypothalamus, 107, **107**, 109, **109**
   lateral, 109
   ventromedial, tumor of, 109
hypothyroidism, 52
hysteria, 20, 25, 143

I
Id, 20, **22**
identity disorder, 137
identity, personal, 21
ideographic method, 18
idiocy, 14
illusion, 63–65, **64**, **65**
   Necker cube, 62, **63**
   Muller-Lyer, **64**, 65
   Ponzo, 64
   size-weight, 65
   trapezoidal window, 64
   wife/mother-in-law, 62
imagery, **82**, 118
immune system, 117
imprinting, 46
impulse control, disorders of, 144
impulsiveness, 51
infancy, 33, 54
infant, brain development of, 33, **34**
   feeding of, 43–44
   intellectual development of, 38–40
   interaction with parent, 44–45
   mental disorders of, 136
   moral development of, 48

motor development of, 41–43
   relationships, 45
   response capability of, 40–41
   response to environment, 45–46
   response to face, 35, **36**, **37**
   response to sound, 36–37
   sleep pattern, **30**, 43
   socialization of, 43–45
   stimulation of, **39**, 45
   visual development of, 34–36
infantile autism, 137
inferiority complex, 21, 123
information processing, 83
inhibition, retroactive, 77
   proactive, 77
inkblot test, **121**
integration, hierarchical, 33
intelligence, 9, 43, 54, 78, 79, 83
   crystallized, 83
   fluid, 83
   test, 79, **79**, 83, 115
   theories of, 18
intoxication, alcohol, 138
introversion, **18**
introvert, 52, **53**
IQ, 79, 80, 83, 136
iris, 34

J
James, William, 15, 17, 34, **35**, 110, 113
James: *Principles of Psychology*, 17
Japanese tea ceremony, **96**
Jesus Christ, **10**
Jung, Carl, **19**, 21, 31, **31**

K
Kagan, Jerome, 51
Klein, Dr. Donald, 120
Klein, Melanie, 21
kleptomania, 144
knowing, 10
Kohler, Wolfgang, 73

L
Laing, R.D., 26
language, 27, **27**, **40**, 54, **57**, **75**, 79, 89, **89**
   braille, **27**
   computer, **27**
   foreign, 78
   Indo-European, **90**
   learning, 98
   learning, by chimpanzee, 90, 93
   sign, **27**
Lapp, **101**
"lateral thinking", 6
learned helplessness, 117
learning, 61, **61**, 65, 66, 68, 69, **71**, **72**,

74, 86
   conditioned, 119
   insight, 73, 75
Leibniz, Gottfried, 13
lens, 34
"life force", 9
"life instinct", 20, 105
limbic system, 106, 109, **109**
linguistics, 6, 27, 98
lips, 91
Locke, John, 34, **35**
Lorenz, Konrad, 106
LSD, 26, **122**
lunacy, 14

M
madness, **9**, **10**, **134**
mainstreaming, 86
manic depressive syndrome, 140
masochism, 144
mathematics, 12, **23**
mechanics, 12
media, influence of, 49, **50**, **51**, 56, 150–151
meditation, **119**
memory, 6, 14, 24, 30, 61, 75–77, 86, 130, 144
   acoustic code of, 76
   effect of mood on, 114
   encoding of, 76, 78
   long term, 76
   loss of, 75, 138
   retrieval, 76, 78
   semantic code of, 76
   short term, 75–76
   storage, 68, 76
   visual code of, 76
manic depressive syndrome, 140
menopause, 108
menstrual cycle, 108
mental illness, **133**, 134–145
mental retardation, 136
mescaline, 26
mesomorph, 53, 55, **55**
metabolism, **111**
Milgram, Stanley, 127
mind, 9
   abnormality of, 14
   conscious, 20, 21
   of infant, 34
   influence of, 12–13
   interaction with natural world, **23**
   preconscious, 20
   unconscious, 20, 21, 25
mirage, **68**
mnemonic system, **76**, **77**
mood disorder, 140
mother, 20, 21
   -infant relationship, 40, **47**, **48**, 52
motivation, 21, 73, 110, 112
   unconscious, 110
   of workers, 146–150

motive, **32**, 65, 66
motor movements, fine, 43
motor movements, gross, 41, 137
Muller-Lyer illusion, **64**
multi-infarct dementia, 138
multiple personality, 144
muscle, 116, 118

N

narcissistic personality disorder, 145
Neanderthal man, 92
neck, 41
Necker cube, 61, **62**
need, 65, 66
nervous system, 69, 118
   central, 25, 139
nerve, vagus, 69
neurology, 15
neuromuscular system, **43**, 49
neurosis, 20, 123, **133**, 134, 140
   hysterical, 24, 143
neuroticism, **18**
neurotransmitter, 25
Newton, Isaac, 12, **12**
non-REM sleep, 137

O

obedience, 128
obesity, 109
object permanence, 39, **40**
obsession, **133**, 141–143
opioids, 138
oppositional disorder, 137
organic affective syndrome, 138
organic brain syndrome, 138–139
organic delusional syndrome, 138
organic mental disorder,
   substance-induced, 138
organizational psychology, 148
orrery, **12**
ovary, 108
overanxious disorder, 136
overeating, 109, 137
oxygen, 116

P

pain, 66
panic attack, 141, 145
panic disorder, 141
paralysis, hysterical, 24
paranoid disorder, 139
paranoid personality disorder, 145
paraphilia, 144
parent, 48, 56, 58
   -child interaction, 44–45, 47, **99**
passive-aggressive personality disorder,
   145
Pavlov, Ivan, 16, 68, 69, **71**

pedophilia, 144
perception, 10, 24, **32**, 61–68
   auditory, 36–37, 38
   cross, 38
   drug-induced distortion of, 26
   field dependence, **52**
   olfactory, 37
   part-whole, **49**
   subliminal, 130–132
   tactile, 37
   taste, 37
   visual, 34–36, 66
perceptual constancy, 63
personality, 50–55, **53**, **55**
   determination of, 10, **32**
   disorder of, **133**, 144–145
   Eysenck model of, **18**
   factor analysis of, 18
   multiple, **133**, 144
   stereotype of, 53
   Type A, 117
pervasive developmental disorder, 137
phencyclidine (PCP), 138
philosophy, 6, 12, 17
phobia, **118**, **133**, 140, 146
phobic reaction, 70
phoneme, 94, 96
phonetic discrimination, 37
phrenology, 15
physics, 12, **23**
Paiget, Jean, 38, **40**, 43, 83
pica, 137
pineal gland, 12, 13
pituitary gland, 52, **111**
planets, influence of, **14**
Plato, 10
play, 43, **44**
play therapy, 145
Ponzo illusion, 64
Popper, Karl, 21, 22, 23, **23**
post-traumatic stress disorder, 143
posture, 97
pragmatism, 17
primary degenerative dementia, 138
productivity, 148–150
psychiatry, 69
psychoanalysis, 19, **19**, 120, 121, **121**,
   146
   neo-Freudian, 21, 22
   object-relations school of, 21
psychodrama, 145
psychodynamic therapy, 146
psychoendocrine immune axis, 118
psychogenic pain disorder, 143
psychogenic amnesia, 144
psychology, 6, **6**, **9**, 14, 69
   comparative, 33
   developmental, 33
   ego, 21
   individual, 21
psychoneurosis, 134
psychosexual disorder, 144
psychosexual dysfunction, 144
psychosis, 26, 121, **133**

paranoid drug-induced, 26
psychosomatics, 116
psychosomatic illness, **133**
psychotherapy, 117–121
   cognitive, 120
   group, 145
   individual, 145
   rational-emotive, 120
puberty, **94**
punishment, 72
pyromania, 144

R

reactive attachment disorder, 136
reading, 83
recall, differential, 130
reflex, 15, 16
   conditioned, 16, 69
   walking, 37, 43
reinforcement, behavioral, 16, 70, 71,
   72, **75**
relationship, development of, 45–46
   interpersonal, 21
relaxation, 118–119, **119**
religion, **6**, 122
religious experience, 15, 17
repression, 20, **20**
retardation, mental, 136
retina, 34, 63
Riley, Vernon, 118
robot, 80
root sentence, 103
rumination disorder of infancy, 137
Russell: *History of Western Philosophy*, 13
Ryle, Gilbert, **13**, 14

S

sadism, 144
satiety center, 109
Schacter, Stanley, 112
schizoid disorder of childhood, 136
schizoid personality disorder, 145
schizophrenia, 24, **25**, 26, 121, 122, **122**,
   133, 139
   paranoid, 26
schizotypal personality disorder, 145
Scientific Monthly, 81
sedative drug, 25
self concept, 56, 58, **58**, **59**
self image, **109**
Seligman, Martin, 117
semantics, 6, 98
semiotics, 6
sensory deprivation, 66
sensory processing, 34
sensory system, 34
sentence, deep structure of, 102–103,
   102
sentence, surface structure of, **102**
separation anxiety, 45

disorder, 136
sex hormone, 52, 55
sexual arousal, 110
sexual attraction, 108
sexual behavior, 97, 108
sexual drive, 20
sexual motivation, 105
Seyle, Hans, 118
shamanistic rite, **10**
shape recognition, 35–36
shaping technique, 70, **73**
shock, therapy, 145
skin, 61
Skinner, Burrhus F., 16, 70, **72**
Skinner box, **72**
Skinner: *Beyond Freedom and Dignity*, 16
skull, 15
sleep, 43
    brain activity during, 28, **28**
    paradoxical, 28
    REM, 28, 30, **30**
    slow-wave, 28, 30
sleep terror disorder, 137
sleepwalking disorder, 137
smell, sense of, 34, 37
smiling, 45, **48**, 57
smoking, 117
sociability, 51
social influence, 53–56
social phobia, 141
socialization, 43–46, 55, 56
socio-cultural bias, 79
Socrates, 9
somatoform disorder, 143
sound, infant response to, 38
specific developmental disorders, 137
speech, 14, 36, 37, 91–92
    categorical perception of, 95
    disorders in children, 137
    Neanderthal, 92
Spearman, Charles, 18
Spielberger, Charles, 114
spinal cord, 110
spirits, possession by, **10**
Spitz, René, 46
stability, **18**
stereotype, 83, 84

behavioral, **56**
    personality, 53, 55
    sexual, 55–56
stereotyped movement disorders, 137
Stern, Daniel, 45
stimulation of infant, **39**, 45–46
    mental, of disadvantaged children, 80
    tactile, 62
stimulus, 16, 34, 38, 61, 66, 68, 70, 81, 110
    tactile, 37
    visual, 35, **66**
stomach, 109
stress, **115**, 117, 118, **119**, **148**
    disorder, post-traumatic, 143
    reaction, **111**, 113
"stressful life events", **113**, 114
stuttering, 137
substance use disorder, 139
successive approximation, 119, 145
sucking, 36, 37, 44, 95
suicide, **116**
Superego, 20, **22**
supernatural, belief in, **127**
symbol, 9, 21, 25, **26**, 27, **40**, 83
symptom, neurotic, 105
syntax, 98–101
syphilis, 24

T
Taoism, 9
taste bud, 34
taste, sense of, 34, 62, **62**, 109
teaching, 47
Teasdale, John, 114
testis, 108
Thanatos, 20
thinking, 43, 54
    convergent, 84
    creative, **82**, 84
    divergent, 84
Thomas, Alexander, 51
Thurstone, Louis, 18
thyroid gland, 52
tic, 137

toilet training, 70
tolerance, drug, 139
tongue, 91–92
training, military, **115**
transference, 120
transsexualism, 144
transvestism, 144
twins, 51, 80
tumor, 109

U
universe, 12, **12**

V
vascular disease and mental illness, 138
vicarious catharsis hypothesis, 151
violence in media, 49, **50**, **51**
vision, 34–36
visual cliff, 35
visual discrimination, 35
vocal chord, 41, 91
voice, infant response to, 36
    pitch of, **97**, 98
voyeurism, 144

W
walking, **43**
    reflex, 37, 43
Watson, John B., 16
weapon, nuclear, **23**
Werner, Heinz, 54
Wernicke's area, 94
whale, 93
witch, 21
withdrawal, 138, 139
Wundt, Wilhelm, 81

Y
Yin and Yang, 9, **9**, 10, 20